Field Guides to Finding a New Career

Internet and Media

The Field Guides to Finding a New Career series

Advertising, Sales, and Marketing

Arts and Entertainment

Education

Film and Television

Food and Culinary Arts

Health Care

Information Technology

Internet and Media

Nonprofits and Government

Outdoor Careers

Field Guides
to Finding a
New Career

Internet and Media

By Amanda Kirk

Ferguson Publishing
An imprint of Infobase Publishing

Field Guides to Finding a New Career: Internet and Media

Copyright © 2009 by Print Matters, Inc.

Ferguson
An imprint of Infobase Publishing
132 West 31st Street
New York, NY 10001

Library of Congress Cataloging-in-Publication Data

Kirk, Amanda.
    Internet and media / by Amanda Kirk.
        p. cm. — (Field guides to finding a new career)
    Includes index.
    ISBN-13: 978-0-8160-7602-4 (hardcover : alk. paper)
    ISBN-10: 0-8160-7602-2 (hardcover : alk. paper)
 1. Internet industry—Vocational guidance—Juvenile literature. 2. Web site development industry—Vocational guidance—Juvenile literature. I. Title.
    HD9696.8.A2K57 2009
    384.3'3023--dc22

                                                           2009012153

Ferguson books are available at special discounts when purchased in bulk quantities for businesses, associations, institutions, or sales promotions. Please call our Special Sales Department in New York at (212) 967-8800 or (800) 322-8755.

You can find Ferguson on the World Wide Web at http://www.fergpubco.com

Produced by Print Matters, Inc.
Text design by A Good Thing, Inc.
Illustrations by Molly Crabapple
Cover design by Takeshi Takahashi

Printed in the United States of America

Bang PMI 10 9 8 7 6 5 4 3 2 1

This book is printed on acid-free paper.

Contents

Introduction: Finding a New Career

Today, changing jobs is an accepted and normal part of life. In fact, according to the Bureau of Labor Statistics, Americans born between 1957 and 1964 held an average of 9.6 jobs from the ages of 18 to 36. The reasons for this are varied: To begin with, people live longer and healthier lives than they did in the past and accordingly have more years of active work life. However, the economy of the twenty-first century is in a state of constant and rapid change, and the workforce of the past does not always meet the needs of the future. Furthermore, fewer and fewer industries provide bonuses such as pensions and retirement health plans, which provide an incentive for staying with the same firm. Other workers experience epiphanies, spiritual growth, or various sorts of personal challenges that lead them to question the paths they have chosen.

Job instability is another prominent factor in the modern workplace. In the last five years, the United States has lost 2.6 *million jobs*; in 2005 alone, 370,000 workers were affected by mass layoffs. Moreover, because of new technology, changing labor markets, ageism, and a host of other factors, many educated, experienced professionals and skilled blue-collar workers have difficulty finding jobs in their former career tracks. Finally—and not just for women—the realities of juggling work and family life, coupled with economic necessity, often force radical revisions of career plans.

No matter how normal or accepted changing careers might be, however, the time of transition can also be a time of anxiety. Faced with the necessity of changing direction in the middle of their journey through life, many find themselves lost. Many career-changers find themselves asking questions such as: Where do I want to go from here? How do I get there? How do I prepare myself for the journey? Thankfully, the Field Guides to Finding a New Career are here to show the way. Using the language and visual style of a travel guide, we show you that reorienting yourself and reapplying your skills and knowledge to a new career is not an uphill slog, but an exciting journey of exploration. No matter whether you are in your twenties or close to retirement age, you can bravely set out to explore new paths and discover new vistas.

Though this series forms an organic whole, each volume is also designed to be a comprehensive, stand-alone, all-in-one guide to getting motivated, getting back on your feet, and getting back to work. We thoroughly discuss common issues such as going back to school, managing your household finances, putting your old skills to work in new situations, and selling yourself to potential employers. Each volume focuses on a broad career field, roughly grouped by Bureau of Labor Statistics' career clusters. Each chapter will focus on a particular career, suggesting new career paths suitable for an individual with that experience and training as well as practical issues involved in seeking and applying for a position.

Many times, the first question career-changers ask is, "Is this new path right for me?" Our self-assessment quiz, coupled with the career compasses at the beginning of each chapter, will help you to match your personal attributes to set you on the right track. Do you possess a storehouse of skilled knowledge? Are you the sort of person who puts others before yourself? Are you methodical and organized? Do you communicate effectively and clearly? Are you good at math? And how do you react to stress? All of these qualities contribute to career success—but they are not equally important in all jobs.

Many career-changers find working for themselves to be more hassle-free and rewarding than working for someone else. However, going at it alone, whether as a self-employed individual or a small-business owner, provides its own special set of challenges. Appendix A, "Going Solo: Starting Your Own Business," is designed to provide answers to many common questions and solutions to everyday problems, from income taxes to accounting to providing health insurance for yourself and your family.

For those who choose to work for someone else, how do you find a job, particularly when you have been out of the labor market for a while? Appendix B, "Outfitting Yourself for Career Success," is designed to answer these questions. It provides not only advice on résumé and self-presentation, but also the latest developments in looking for jobs, such as online resources, headhunters, and placement agencies. Additionally, it recommends how to explain an absence from the workforce to a potential employer.

Changing careers can be stressful, but it can also be a time of exciting personal growth and discovery. We hope that the Field Guides to Finding a New Career not only help you get your bearings in today's employment jungle, but set you on the path to personal fulfillment, happiness, and prosperity.

How to Use This Book

Career Compasses

Each chapter begins with a series of "career compasses" to help you get your bearings and determine if this job is right for you, based on your answers to the self-assessment quiz at the beginning of the book. Does it require a mathematical mindset? Communication skills? Organizational skills? If you're not a "people person," a job requiring you to interact with the public might not be right for you. On the other hand, your organizational skills might be just what are needed in the back office.

Destination

A brief overview, giving you and introduction to the career, briefly explaining what it is, its advantages, why it is so satisfying, its growth potential, and its income potential.

You Are Here

A self-assessment asking you to locate yourself on your journey. Are you working in a related field? Are you working in a field where some skills will transfer? Or are you doing something completely different? In each case, we suggest ways to reapply your skills, gain new ones, and launch yourself on your new career path.

Navigating the Terrain

To help you on your way, we have provided a handy map showing the stages in your journey to a new career. "Navigating the Terrain" will show you the road you need to follow to get where you are going. Since the answers are not the same for everyone and every career, we are sure to show how there are multiple ways to get to the same destination.

Organizing Your Expedition

Fleshing out "Navigating the Terrain," we give explicit directions on how to enter this new career: Decide on a destination, scout the terrain, and decide on a path that is right for you. Of course, the answers are not the same for everyone.

Landmarks

People have different needs at different ages. "Landmarks" presents advice specific to the concerns of each age demographic: early career (twenties), mid-career (thirties to forties), senior employees (fifties) and second-career starters (sixties). We address not only issues such as overcoming age discrimination, but also possible concerns of spouses and families (for instance, paying college tuition with reduced income) and keeping up with new technologies.

Essential Gear

Indispensable tips for career-changers on things such as gearing your résumé to a job in a new field, finding contacts and networking, obtaining further education and training, and how to gain experience in the new field.

Notes from the Field

Sometimes it is useful to consult with those who have gone before for insights and advice. "Notes from the Field" presents interviews with career-changers, presenting motivations and methods that you can identify with.

Further Resources

Finally, we give a list of "expedition outfitters" to provide you with further resources and trade resources.

Make the Most of Your Journey

Just as the industrial revolution changed the job market and, with it, the standard of living of the industrialized world, the technological revolution has once again changed the way we live and the career possibilities open to us. We have come a long way from a crank-up Model T Ford to a hybrid vehicles in which kids can watch DVDs in the backseat as you follow the GPS instructions to your destination. It is not just the number of new technologies available to us that is creating new types of jobs, there is also the fact that technology is advancing faster every day, with the time decreasing rapidly between a technology's adoption and its obsolescence. Employment opportunities abound today in industries that may not have existed when you began your career. The advent of the Internet with its World Wide Web has added a completely new sector to the economy. In this volume, you will find an overview of some of the Internet-related jobs that are available. Some of these careers, such as animator and day trader, are in industries that existed before the Internet but that have changed and adapted to utilize computers. Other jobs, such as Web producer, Web entrepreneur and e-business specialist, are practically new fields. Still other jobs, such as game designer, Web master, Web designer, eBay seller, and blogger, did not exist at all before the Internet.

Animators have been around since prehistoric man drew extra legs on cave paintings of animals to convey the idea of motion. The flip books of the nineteenth century were a slightly more sophisticated attempt at animation, a field that came into its own with the invention of the camera and motion picture. With their ability to draw cels, animators certainly did not need the Internet, but computers have completely changed the art form. Some animators still draw by hand and scan their creations into a computer, but the vast majority use the computer as their drawing tool. The art form has changed irrevocably, and computers have greatly increased the variety of types of animation and its possibilities. Furthermore, a large portion of the market for today's animated films is adults, so aspiring animators are not limited to children's fare.

Likewise, stock trading was a thriving business long before the invention of the modern computer but the ability to trade in real time over the Internet has gotten rid of the middleman and allowed armchair traders to work from home. Specialized software eliminates the need to deal directly with a broker over the phone, and enables day traders to trade in markets on exchanges worldwide. The speed with which information reaches the day trader has revolutionized the stock market. There is certainly risk involved in this field, but the convenience, the challenge, and the potential, however small, for wealth, continue to lure the risk takers among us.

A producer used to be the person who bankrolled a production, such as a film or Broadway show. Now, the term is used to describe the person who brings together all the elements of a production, whether or not he or she is funding it. A Web producer changes the meaning of the term yet again. This new field can be seen as akin to a webmaster: that is, the person who is in charge of managing all of the elements of the Web site, bringing it all together. This dynamic career requires a diverse skill set. A Web producer will be expected to possess both design and technical skills, as well as public relations and marketing savvy, and varying degrees of management skills, depending upon the company. This is a good career choice for someone who likes to continually work on new projects and in new environments.

In fact, Web producer and webmaster are such similar professions that one will often find the titles used interchangeably in job ads. The webmaster's job did not exist before the popularity of the Internet brought with it a plethora of Web sites that needed to be created and updated. Virtually every business and government entity has a Web site these days, and it is the webmasters who keep them functional and current. Webmasters usually possess design and coding skills. Some work alone to maintain a Web site, others supervise a team. All webmasters must have strong technical skills and a good design sense.

A closely related profession to webmaster is that of Web designer. Webmasters often start out as Web designers and change titles when they assume responsibilities that extend beyond the initial design of a Web site. Most Web designers can do at least some of their own coding, and fall somewhere along a spectrum from glorified graphic designers with limited technical skills to fully-fledged programmers with some modicum of design sense.

The Internet has created opportunities for businesses to expand their customer base beyond their local area or even to eliminate a brick-and-mortar presence altogether and operate with a purely digital storefront. Web entrepreneurs are cut from the same cloth as the old offline sort, they just bring technical knowledge and Web marketing savvy to their already bold and impressive list of talents. Starting an online business can be easier and more straightforward than starting a "brick-and-mortar" one, but it still requires a significant amount of start-up capital, hard work, and confidence.

Business management has long since become a distinct profession, with the MBA degree setting the standards for expected skills. Rather than valuing industry-specific knowledge, companies have come to respect general business management skills that can be applied to a variety of industries. The Internet has broadened opportunities for managerial types and it is a growing area of specialization that is infiltrating management education. MBA candidates and B.A. business majors can now specialize in e-business, and computer scientists who aspire to a management position can become e-business IT specialists. This growing field may provide an interesting career option for the business manager looking for a new challenge.

Speaking of challenges, the gamers out there who are always trying to take it to the next level have a chance to put their imaginations and technical skills to the test designing innovative games for the burgeoning video game market. The job is not all play and no work. Contrary to popular belief, game designers do not, in fact, spend all day playing video games. Many are animators who are hard at work on the graphics, some work exclusively with sound effects, some are programmers who code (and code and code), and others are members of the design team who perform their specific roles in the production process to bring the next game sensation to your computer.

Another career that would not exist without computers is the eBay seller. Actually, it is a bit misleading to call this a career. EBay has many casual sellers who do not earn significant amounts of their income from the site. Other eBay sellers are business owners who augment their sales by offering some of their merchandise on eBay, but very few sellers make a living exclusively from eBay sales. Up until 2008, this was a somewhat viable option, but the online auction site has fallen on hard times, in part as a result of its own poor policy choices, and it is losing market share. The recent economic downturn has not helped. Nonetheless, selling merchandise on eBay is still a good move for some businesses, and may provide an additional source of income for you.

Another online occupation that cannot honestly be referred to as a career possibility is blogger. Online journals, or blogs, have grown exponentially in popularity, and there are probably several that you have bookmarked and read on a regular basis. The types of blogs out there are nearly as varied as their number, which by some calculations is over 300 million. Though you may occasionally read about "blog-to-book" deals, very few paying positions exist for bloggers. You might find blogging to be fun, useful for PR for your business, or even therapeutic, but you are unlikely to be able to make a living at it.

There are other possible careers in new media that take advantage of the rapid growth of the Internet and related communications and graphics technologies, but the ten professions profiled in this volume should give you a good sense of some popular options and, most importantly, offer you some sound advice on how to harness your education and experience to help you launch successfully into a new career.

Self-Assessment Quiz

I: Relevant Knowledge

1. How many years of specialized training have you had?
    (a) None, it is not required
    (b) Several weeks to several months of training
    (c) A year-long course or other preparation
    (d) Years of preparation in graduate or professional school,
         or equivalent job experience

2. Would you consider training to obtain certification or other required
    credentials?
    (a) No
    (b) Yes, but only if it is legally mandated
    (c) Yes, but only if it is the industry standard
    (d) Yes, if it is helpful (even if not mandatory)

3. In terms of achieving success, how would rate the following
    qualities in order from least to most important?
    (a) ability, effort, preparation
    (b) ability, preparation, effort
    (c) preparation, ability, effort
    (d) preparation, effort, ability

4. How would you feel about keeping track of current developments
    in your field?
    (a) I prefer a field where very little changes
    (b) If there were a trade publication, I would like to keep
         current with that
    (c) I would be willing to regularly recertify my credentials
         or learn new systems
    (d) I would be willing to aggressively keep myself up-to-date in a
         field that changes constantly

5. For whatever reason, you have to train a bright young successor to do your job. How quickly will he or she pick it up?
    (a) Very quickly
    (b) He or she can pick up the necessary skills on the job
    (c) With the necessary training he or she should succeed with hard work and concentration
    (d) There is going to be a long breaking-in period—there is no substitute for experience

II: Caring

1. How would you react to the following statement: "Other people are the most important thing in the world?"
    (a) No! Me first!
    (b) I do not really like other people, but I do make time for them
    (c) Yes, but you have to look out for yourself first
    (d) Yes, to such a degree that I often neglect my own well-being

2. Who of the following is the best role model?
    (a) Ayn Rand
    (b) Napoléon Bonaparte
    (c) Bill Gates
    (d) Florence Nightingale

3. How do you feel about pets?
    (a) I do not like animals at all
    (b) Dogs and cats and such are OK, but not for me
    (c) I have a pet, or I wish I did
    (d) I have several pets, and caring for them occupies significant amounts of my time

4. Which of the following sets of professions seems most appealing to you?
    (a) business leader, lawyer, entrepreneur
    (b) politician, police officer, athletic coach
    (c) teacher, religious leader, counselor
    (d) nurse, firefighter, paramedic

5. How well would you have to know someone to give them $100 in a harsh but not life-threatening circumstance? It would have to be...
    (a) ...a close family member or friend (brother or sister, best friend)
    (b) ...a more distant friend or relation (second cousin, coworkers)
    (c) ...an acquaintance (a coworker, someone from a community organization or church)
    (d) ...a complete stranger

III: Organizational Skills

1. Do you create sub-folders to further categorize the items in your "Pictures" and "Documents" folders on your computer?
    (a) No
    (b) Yes, but I do not use them consistently
    (c) Yes, and I use them consistently
    (d) Yes, and I also do so with my e-mail and music library

2. How do you keep track of your personal finances?
    (a) I do not, and I am never quite sure how much money is in my checking account
    (b) I do not really, but I always check my online banking to make sure I have money
    (c) I am generally very good about budgeting and keeping track of my expenses, but sometimes I make mistakes
    (d) I do things such as meticulously balance my checkbook, fill out Excel spreadsheets of my monthly expenses, and file my receipts

3. Do you systematically order commonly used items in your kitchen?
    (a) My kitchen is a mess
    (b) I can generally find things when I need them
    (c) A place for everything, and everything in its place
    (d) Yes, I rigorously order my kitchen and do things like alphabetize spices and herbal teas

4. How do you do your laundry?
    (a) I cram it in any old way
    (b) I separate whites and colors

    (c)   I separate whites and colors, plus whether it gets dried

    (d)   Not only do I separate whites and colors and drying or non-drying, I organize things by type of clothes or some other system

5. Can you work in clutter?

    (a)   Yes, in fact I feel energized by the mess

    (b)   A little clutter never hurt anyone

    (c)   No, it drives me insane

    (d)   Not only does my workspace need to be neat, so does that of everyone around me

IV: Communication Skills

1. Do people ask you to speak up, not mumble, or repeat yourself?

    (a)   All the time

    (b)   Often

    (c)   Sometimes

    (d)   Never

2. How do you feel about speaking in public?

    (a)   It terrifies me

    (b)   I can give a speech or presentation if I have to, but it is awkward

    (c)   No problem!

    (d)   I frequently give lectures and addresses, and I am very good at it

3. What's the difference between *their, they're,* and *there*?

    (a)   I do not know

    (b)   I know there is a difference, but I make mistakes in usage

    (c)   I know the difference, but I can not articulate it

    (d)   *Their* is the third-person possessive, *they're* is a contraction for *they are,* and *there is* a deictic adverb meaning "in that place"

4. Do you avoid writing long letters or e-mails because you are ashamed of your spelling, punctuation, and grammatical mistakes?

    (a)   Yes

    (b)   Yes, but I am either trying to improve or just do not care what people think

    (c)   The few mistakes I make are easily overlooked

    (d)   Save for the occasional typo, I do not ever make mistakes in usage

5.   Which choice best characterizes the most challenging book you are willing to read in your spare time?

    (a)   I do not read

    (b)   Light fiction reading such as the Harry Potter series, *The Da Vinci Code*, or mass-market paperbacks

    (c)   Literary fiction or mass-market nonfiction such as history or biography

    (d)   Long treatises on technical, academic, or scientific subjects

V: Mathematical Skills

1.   Do spreadsheets make you nervous?

    (a)   Yes, and I do not use them at all

    (b)   I can perform some simple tasks, but I feel that I should leave them to people who are better-qualified than myself

    (c)   I feel that I am a better-than-average spreadsheet user

    (d)   My job requires that I be very proficient with them

2.   What is the highest level math class you have ever taken?

    (a)   I flunked high-school algebra

    (b)   Trigonometry or pre-calculus

    (c)   College calculus or statistics

    (d)   Advanced college mathematics

3.   Would you rather make a presentation in words or using numbers and figures?

    (a)   Definitely in words

    (b)   In words, but I could throw in some simple figures and statistics if I had to

    (c)   I could strike a balance between the two

    (d)   Using numbers as much as possible; they are much more precise

4.   Cover the answers below with a sheet of paper, and then solve the following word problem: Mary has been legally able to vote for exactly half her life. Her husband John is three years older than she. Next year,

their son Harvey will be exactly one-quarter of John's age. How old was Mary when Harvey was born?

(a) I couldn't work out the answer

(b) 25

(c) 26

(d) 27

5. Cover the answers below with a sheet of paper, and then solve the following word problem: There are seven children on a school bus. Each child has seven book bags. Each bag has seven big cats in it. Each cat has seven kittens. How many legs are there on the bus?

(a) I couldn't work out the answer

(b) 2,415

(c) 16,821

(d) 10,990

VI: Ability to Manage Stress

1. It is the end of the working day, you have 20 minutes to finish an hour-long job, and you are scheduled to pick up your children. Your supervisor asks you why you are not finished. You:

(a) Have a panic attack

(b) Frantically redouble your efforts

(c) Calmly tell her you need more time, make arrangements to have someone else pick up the kids, and work on the project past closing time

(d) Calmly tell her that you need more time to do it right and that you have to leave, or ask if you can release this flawed version tonight

2. When you are stressed, do you tend to:

(a) Feel helpless, develop tightness in your chest, break out in cold sweats, or have other extreme, debilitating physiological symptoms?

(b) Get irritable and develop a hair-trigger temper, drink too much, obsess over the problem, or exhibit other "normal" signs of stress?

(c) Try to relax, keep your cool, and act as if there is no problem

(d) Take deep, cleansing breaths and actively try to overcome the feelings of stress

3. The last time I was so angry or frazzled that I lost my composure was:
   (a) Last week or more recently
   (b) Last month
   (c) Over a year ago
   (d) So long ago I cannot remember

4. Which of the following describes you?
   (a) Stress is a major disruption in my life, people have spoken to me about my anger management issues, or I am on medication for my anxiety and stress
   (b) I get anxious and stressed out easily
   (c) Sometimes life can be a challenge, but you have to climb that mountain!
   (d) I am generally easygoing

5. What is your ideal vacation?
   (a) I do not take vacations; I feel my work life is too demanding
   (b) I would just like to be alone, with no one bothering me
   (c) I would like to do something not too demanding, like a cruise, with friends and family
   (d) I am an adventurer; I want to do exciting (or even dangerous) things and visit foreign lands

Scoring:

For each category...

For every answer of *a*, add zero points to your score.
For every answer of *b*, add ten points to your score.
For every answer of *c*, add fifteen points to your score.
For every answer of *d*, add twenty points to your score.

The result is your percentage in that category.

Web Producer

Web Producer

Career Compasses

Get your bearings on what it takes to be a successful Web producer.

Relevant Knowledge of Web design and project management (25%)

Organizational Skills to write up project plans and coordinate production (25%)

Communication Skills to deal with your team effectively (20%)

Ability to Manage Stress is key to handling the pressures of managing a team and pleasing the client (30%)

Destination: Web Producer

If you have pulled an oar as a Web designer, marketer, engineer, editor, or any other Web-related discipline, and you think that you are ready to be captain of the ship, then a career as a Web producer may be right for you. A Web producer is the harried individual who coordinates all of the elements that go into building a successful Web site. He or she draws up project plans and directs the team that will take the Web site from idea to cyber-reality.

Most Web producers get their start as a member of the Web design team and work their way up to a management position. It is crucial that you have some knowledge and experience of building Web sites before you are in charge of doing so for paying clients. Some jobs that would lead to a viable transition to Web producer include Web designer, e-business specialist, Web marketing and advertising positions, Web manager, Web content writer or editor, Web engineer or coder, user interface tester, and any assistant roles in Web production. It may be possible to parlay project management experience from another field into a Web producer position, but you will have to convince potential employers that your skills are directly transferable to the Web arena. Deadlines are usually tight, so the learning curve will be steep. Without germane prior experience, it is unlikely that being a Web producer is a viable career option. If you choose to go back to school to acquire relevant skills, you will most likely have to take an entry-level job as a member of the production team and work your way up to the producer role.

Essential Gear

Carry your portfolio in your carry-on. The first thing any potential employer is going to want to see is your previous work. Creating an online portfolio of Web sites that you have worked on is crucial to securing a Web production job. No one is going to hire you until they see what you can do. Your portfolio should feature the Web sites of which you are most proud, and also demonstrate variety of styles and functionality. You can create separate portfolios for different job applications to target them to what each potential employer is seeking.

Another career from which Web producers frequently hail is journalism. Most media companies maintain a Web site, whether they are primarily television or radio stations, newspapers or magazines. Typically, a journalist is assigned to produce the online content. The Web site of a television show may contain episodes of the show as well as providing a peek behind the scenes at the cast and crew. The purpose of the site might be primarily PR, to generate interest in the show, or to provide a place for fans to watch episodes, interviews, and additional material. The Web producer would work closely with the show's other production staff to determine appropriate content for the online medium. In the case of a revenue-generating Web site, the Web producer may be responsible for displaying merchandise, updating prices and inventory, or managing advertising space. Depending on the size of the staff, this could be primarily supervisory or it could be hands-on, hence the wide range of potential skills for this job. A related concern for the Web producer is creating interest in a Web site—generating traffic. This is a crucial aspect of the job if the Web site relies on advertising revenue. In this respect, online production resembles its "real world" counterpart.

It can be tricky to distinguish the role of a Web producer from the other jobs involved in creating a Web site. There are several reasons for this, but the main one is that production is not always considered a distinct job function. There are three separate ingredients in the design of a Web site: the content, the design, and the programming. Each of those elements requires distinct skills. The people who write the content may have no idea how to format and style it for the Web and the programmers who code and build the site may lack any design sense of how to lay it out. In theory, a Web producer brings these disparate elements together to produce a cohesive Web site. In reality, many Web sites are made by individuals who combine these three roles in some way. A designer, for example, may program the site as well as lay it out visually, or the content provider may decide how to present his or her work and use software to code it on his or her own. In this way production can happen without it being a distinct job. A Web site has to have a substantial budget for someone to be in charge of production alone. This also explains why Web producers generally start out as designers or programmers or, sometimes, content providers, and move into a production-only role when the opportunity arises.

Some other titles that you will see used in job advertisements for Web producers include online producer, content producer, and online editor.

Essential Gear

Pack your technical skills for the trip. A great design sense will carry you far, and portfolio of beautiful sites with impressive special effects will certainly help you land a job, but keeping that new job will involve having the Web site development skills to put your ideas into action. In previous positions, you may have been able to rely on programmers to implement your designs. Before you embark on a new employment adventure, make sure that you know how much technical support you can expect and ensure that you are crystal clear on how much technical knowledge your new employer expects you to possess.

Those names give you a sense that a producer is ultimately responsible for every aspect of a Web site: how it looks, how it functions, and what it says. A Web site usually contains some text, some images, and, increasingly, video and audio content. The producer is primarily concerned with the content, and overall look and feel of a Web site, and so is slightly more likely to have a content-writing or design background than a technical background. That is not to say that programmers and HTML coders do not work their way up to Web production positions, but traditionally, those on the technical side are less likely to concern themselves with the big picture. Designers often have to master some technical skills in order to know what is possible and how to get various visual effects, and low-budget content providers may post their own content online without the aid of technical assistance, making these two roles slightly more likely to develop into Web production. A true Web producer works with both designers and developers, focusing on the character of the Web site and keeping its appearance and content fresh and up-to-date.

You Are Here

You can begin your journey to Web producing from many different locales.

Do you have experience in Web design? The field of Web production grew, in part, from the field of Web design as designers realized that they needed to know some programming. Some Web designers began their careers as graphic designers, studying graphic design at a time when design was just becoming computer-based. The level of technical knowledge expected of designers has increased exponentially through the years, to the point where designers are calling themselves Web producers because they are capable of designing and coding a Web site by themselves, without the assistance of programmers. If you are already a Web designer, you will have the easiest transition into your new field.

Are you involved in marketing or PR? The ultimate responsibility for generating traffic to a Web site falls to the producer. Web producers need to keep on top of the latest technology and trends, and keep their Web sites fresh, innovative and interactive to attract and retain users. The importance of design, content generating, and coding skills has already been emphasized. Add to that marketing savvy and we are getting closer to the full skill set expected of a Web producer. If you are trying to enter this field, a marketing or PR background can help you get your first gig.

Do you have a new media background? Following on from the last point, Web sites are primarily a new way to sell stuff and disseminate information. This new medium is distinct from other media, and a background in another medium, such as newspapers, does not automatically translate into the ability to design and mount a useful Web site for a news outlet. Potential employers will want to see that you have worked extensively online and that you are familiar and comfortable in this environment.

Organizing Your Expedition

Before you set out, know where you are going.

Decide on a destination. The duties of Web producers depend upon the size and type of company for which they work. In small companies, the Web producer may be expected to act as designer, content provider, and developer. At the other extreme, the Web producer may function essentially as a project manager, with a team of designers, content providers, and coders. In some firms, the work may be repetitive, with little more than updates to a site required. Other jobs will demand that you produce Web sites with a variety of content, style, and functionality, and require that you continue your education to keep your skill set and design sense up-to-date. You might want to start by considering how much of the work of Web site creation you are able and willing to do on your own. Your skills and interests will steer you in the direction of appropriate jobs.

Scout the terrain. Once you have a sense of the size and type of firm that appeals to you, look at some job advertisements to get an idea of what degrees, work experience, and skills are being sought. Pay careful attention to the nature and scope of the position. Web production is a

Navigating the Terrain

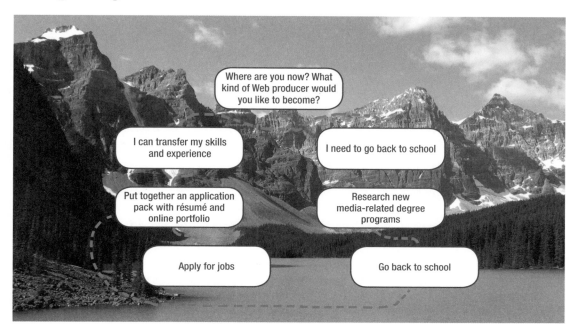

Where are you now? What kind of Web producer would you like to become?

I can transfer my skills and experience

I need to go back to school

Put together an application pack with résumé and online portfolio

Research new media-related degree programs

Apply for jobs

Go back to school

new enough field that there is a tremendous variety in what different employers seek. Ensure that the scope of the duties is a good match for your skills and interests, and that the compensation is appropriate for the level and breadth of work involved. If you know of companies for which you might like to work that are not currently hiring, schedule an informational interview. Ask if they are willing to evaluate your portfolio and give you some personal advice on how to bolster your appeal to potential employers. Above all, do not get discouraged: The right job is out there if you are resourceful and persistent.

Find the path that is right for you. Web producers work in a variety of organizational environments. Some work for the public sector at various government agencies, others for large corporations that choose to do their Web production in-house. Most Web producers work for design agencies where they lead projects for clients, sometimes in their own offices but occasionally farmed out to work long-term for clients in their fa-

Notes from the Field
Mimi Kantor
Interactive producer
Boston, Massachusetts

What were you doing before you decided to change careers?

I was taking any job that came along that sounded kind of fun, but this practice was not providing me with a career trajectory. I had worked in special events, film, photography, and marketing but really wasn't going anywhere.

Why did you change your career?

I needed to create a future for myself that would allow me to have some creative freedom, satisfy my pragmatic need to earn a living and become more stable in my professional goals. My career change was deliberate and thoughtful. I wanted something that would combine all of my past experiences into something that was more cohesive.

How did you make the transition?

I decided to go back to school and get a M.A. in media studies and film. For me, the M.A. was helpful in terms of learning general soft-

cilities. How many hats you wear depends upon the size of the agency. If the agency is small, you might participate in sales and marketing, drumming up your own clients. You may need to cover some administrative tasks if the agency is not large enough to have a separate staff for all such functions. The larger the agency, the more specialized your role will be, and the more time you will be able to devote to your primary occupation of Web production. Some Web producers work as independent consultants. This is slightly more difficult to do as a producer than as a designer since you must work with a team, but it is a viable option in certain circumstances. Since Web production opportunities are ubiquitous to all industries and sectors of the economy thanks to the need for everyone and their dog to have a sophisticated Web site, consider the type of organization in which you would like to work, and whether you think you can go it alone as a consultant.

ware and the relationships amongst media as well as gaining a clear understanding of how to create digitally. It has not really helped me get a job, unlike an MBA or JD, which might have been the clear ticket to being hired. Pushing aside my ego and salary requirements to gain work experience and staying diligently on the path has been my most beneficial ally. I have gained work experience by networking and freelancing for several years. After two years of freelancing I am finally in the right position to transition to a full-time position at a great company. One recruiter I spoke to said it best, "You think things through and know what to do, but don't have the notches on your belt yet."

What are the keys to success in your new career?

Continual re-education and paying attention to current technology, philosophy, and trends. The interactive industry is so changeable that keeping current is one of the best ways to stay ahead of the game. And in this particular case, being a generalist in all matters media is extremely helpful.

Go back to school. Like most new media jobs, Web production is a field where skills and experience count more than degrees. If you have the requisite skills, and a résumé and portfolio to prove it, most employers will not care what you majored in. It is one of those fields where what counts is that you are the best applicant at the job, with the most relevant skills and experience. But if you are reading this because you are considering segueing into Web production from another field, it stands to reason that you might not have all the skills and experience you need to make that move. In that case, a relevant degree is a good place to start the process of building a résumé and portfolio that will get you into your desired field. If you already have a bachelor's degree in an unrelated field, you can still move straight into a master's in media studies. This is probably your most direct route to a Web production job. You can also look into programs in graphic design, marketing (with a program emphasis on online marketing), and journalism.

Landmarks

If you are in your twenties . . . Think first about education, then job experience. At your age, employers will be looking first to see if you have a relevant degree, so choose an appropriate major if you are still in school or consider going back to school for a masters in media studies or another one of the related fields described above. Start building a portfolio now, even if you have to design Web sites for free at first.

If you are in your thirties or forties . . . Build on the advice to twenty-somethings above. First consider your educational qualifications, and augment them if necessary. At this stage of your life, it may be more feasible for you to return to school part-time while you keep your current job. Employers will be expecting a larger portfolio, with more variety, considering that you have been in the workforce longer. If your portfolio is thin, you may need to look around for opportunities to volunteer to design some Web sites. This is a good time to use your network of family, friends, and community organizations to which you belong.

If you are in your fifties . . . The path into the field of Web production is similar regardless of age. You will need to demonstrate to potential employers that you have the educational qualifications, relevant experience, and design skills to stand out from the other applicants. Your age is not really relevant, except that older workers still sometimes face the assumption that younger employers have better technical skills and are more in touch with online media and marketing. You may have to work harder to prove your suitability for the job, but do not let that stop you from pursuing this career change.

If you are over sixty . . . There is little to add to the advice given above for other age groups, except that you may have more financial flexibility if you have a pension or retirement savings that could serve as income whilst you design Web sites on a volunteer basis to boost your portfolio, obtain an internship to bolster your skills, or return to school.

Further Resources

Website Production Management Techniques from Macromedia. Obviously, their information preferences their own software, but it is still useful. There are many forums in which you can ask questions and read archived advice.   http://www.adobe.com/resources/techniques

Education-Portal.com provides more information than you ever wanted to know about media studies degrees, including lists of top schools.   http://education-portal.com/media_studies_degree.html

New Media Bytes is a Web site dedicated to providing the latest information about the transition of the news media to an online format. http://www.newmediabytes.com

Web Producers Organization (WPO) is a professional membership organization for Web producers and related jobs. Their Web site includes a job board.   http://webproducers.org

Game Designer

Game Designer

Career Compasses

Get your bearings on what it takes to be a successful game designer.

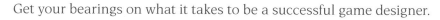

Relevant Knowledge of the game industry market (50%)

Organizational Skills to keep track of the minute details of each game as you build it level by level, and of the many different parts that go into the finished product (20%)

Mathematical Skills are usually a sign of a mind suited to computer work (20%)

Ability to Manage Stress is key to handling the pressure of deadlines and the risk that a game will not take off in the marketplace (10%)

Destination: Game Designer

Do you want the good news or the bad news first? Let us start with the good news: Yes, you can make a living—a great living, in some cases—as a designer of video games, and it is a bit like a kid being invited to work in the candy store. The bad news—and this may come as a shock—is that video game designers do not get to play video games at work (much). They are too busy dreaming up new games, and doing the work involved in making those games, to play with existing games on their work time. Designing a video game involves creativity, communication among a design team, and a vast assortment of technical skills. It is like the difference between sitting in the audience at a movie and being part of the team that put it together. The set dressers, painters, designers, lighting experts, sound technicians, makeup artists, costume designers, editors, and cinematographers each perform one small and distinct behind-the-scenes task to make the film come together on the reel that reaches your local cinema. They perform that same task, over and over, on each new film. Sure, actors may turn to directing once they have the Hollywood clout, but gaffers do not suddenly do makeup on their next film and set dressers do not act. So, if you have been following this analogy, you can see that game design is no more like game playing than watching a movie is like making one. If you are still intrigued by the idea of making games as a career, read on for more detailed information on how to make this career change.

Essential Gear

Prepare a perceptive portfolio of prototypes. Potential employers want only one thing: for their games to make money. Show them that you understand the industry by preparing a portfolio of game prototypes that are targeted to the market demographic in which the company specializes. Demonstrate that you know what game characteristics appeal to each type of game buyer and back up your claims with statistics. The better prepared you are, and the more ideas you present and energy you can radiate, the more likely you are to get the job.

You Are Here

You can begin your journey to game designing from many different locales.

Do you love to play video games? Of course you do: That is why you want to make new games for a living. But when you play games, do you keep thinking of ways that you could improve them? Do you have ideas for new games, and for new iterations of existing games? Does thinking about video games, not just the act of playing them, excite your creativity?

Do you have a related degree? If you have an educational background in computer programming, animation, graphic design, or some aspects of the film industry, you are well placed to segue into the field of game design. If not, consider seriously whether you can commit to two to four years of school before you launch your new career. The technical demands of this field of high and exacting; you cannot fake it, and playing games may make you rich or a hero in the cyberverse but it does not translate into marketable skills in the real world.

Do you work in a related industry? Above all, remember that video game design is work. You are not, contrary to popular belief, sitting around *playing* video games all day. Just because you enjoy playing them does not necessarily mean that you will like the technical work involved in designing them. If you have done related software development, animation, or worked in some aspect of the computer or film industry, you may have a better idea if the work suits you. If not, take some courses first to find your niche in the array of skill sets that contribute to a finished game product.

Organizing your Expedition

Before you set out, know where you are going.

Decide on a destination. There are a lot of choices to make as the path to a new career forks, and forks again. The first intersection you will come to in the video game industry involves the size of the company. This has a major impact on type of work that you would do there. In a large company, many employees work on a given game, each one handling only a small part of it with a highly specialized job. This might be a good option for you if you have one relevant skill that you hope to parlay into a game design career, if you like working on large teams, or if you are interested in focusing closely on one aspect of game design. At a small or even medium size company, fewer employees will work on one game, necessitating that each performs a variety of technical and design tasks. If you want more input in the design process or you have a range of skills that you would like to utilize, this may be a better environment for you. The next fork in the road occurs over the target audience for the games. Larger companies deal in blander, mass-market games that sell to huge consumer bases. Smaller companies may specialize in games using certain technologies, styles, or platforms, and that are marketed

Navigating the Terrain

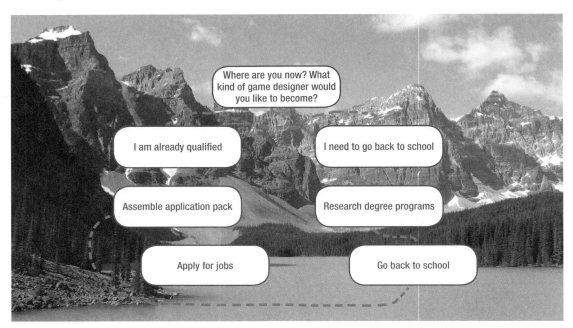

to women or girls, men or boys. Games are usually finely targeted to one demographic, so be sure the company for which you choose to work designs games for a market demographic that you can relate to and for which you enjoy designing. If you like graphically violent games, you may not be happy designing games pitched to the female gamer.

Scout the terrain. The next step after deciding on a target company size and game market is to see what jobs are available in your area. The work environment in this industry is casual, and many designers can work from home or telecommute; nonetheless, your employment options may be more limited if you do not live near many video game design companies. Think carefully about whether you are willing and able to move for the right job.

Find the path that is right for you. The key to career contentment is matching your talents, skills, and interests with lucrative work. Video game design seems like a no-brainer as a dream job, more like getting paid to play than work. Yet, as noted above, it is work. Designers are not playing games; they are generating ideas, conducting market research, and fiddling with technical aspects of future games that can be frustrating, often while working under a tight deadline. So, consider carefully what about the *actual work* of game design appeals to you rather than just what about *playing* video games does.

Go back to school. Top-rated video game design schools include the ITT Technical Institute, DeVry University, the Art Institute of Pittsburgh—Online Division, and the Art Institutes. The ITT Technical Institute has over 100 campuses nationwide. Its School of Drafting and Design offers a bachelor's degree in Digital Entertainment and Game Design. In addition to general education courses that are necessary for any bachelor's degree, students in this program study the entire game design process, including animation, level design, and the latest gaming technology. DeVry University also has campuses nationwide and offers online courses. It offers a bachelor's degree in Game and Simulation Programming. This program is application oriented and prepares graduates for a variety of software development roles, such as programmer, software engineer and project coordinator. Students undertake coursework in the mathematics and physics of games, game design, modifications (MOD), and learn the fundamentals of programming as well as programming applied to massively multi-player online games (MMOG), two- and three-dimensional graphics programming, simulation, and game engine design. The Art Institute of Pittsburgh—Online Division is a convenient choice wherever you live. Their focus is heavily on the artistic rather than the programming side of game design. Courses in their online Game Art and Design bachelor's degree program include such subjects as game design strategies, 3-D animation, motion capture, visual storytelling, character development, scene and set design, low-polygon modeling, level design, and texture mapping. The Art Institutes, named in the plural because there are many of them around the country (check them out here: http://www.artinstitutes.edu/), have a Game Art and Design Program at several campuses. Westwood College has several campuses in southern California and the Denver area, as well as a Chicago outpost. It offers bacheloris degrees in Game Art and Design and Game Software Development. Its curriculum includes courses in management as well as 3-D modeling and animation, cinematography, and color theory. There

Notes from the Field

Stephen B. Lewis
Chief creative officer
San Francisco, California

What were you doing before you decided to change careers?

Previously I billed myself as an animator for games, though I did a lot of 3-D modeling, texture painting, conceptual design, and user interface for the various game companies I worked for. Basically I did anything that involved art production for games.

Why did you change your career?

I'm more of a generalist in the sense that I like to do a bit of everything in the art pipeline, but the game industry has evolved to rely more and more on specialists. Large game companies tend to hire specifically for a modeler, or an animator, but not necessarily someone to do both. Because I get bored doing the same thing over and over I usually found work at very small companies and/or on very small teams where I would have to wear many hats by necessity. Even so, I was usually left feeling unfulfilled working on other people's games. But nobody at any of these companies was handing me the keys to the car, so to speak. I was always just an artist/animator.

How did you make the transition?

When I started working at my last company I was one of 11 employees and the only artist. Four years later they were up to about 100 employees and I was starting to feel like a cog in the machine. It was then that I began working on a game prototype with a couple friends in my spare time on nights and weekends. It was liberating to have so much more say and control over what I was doing in my side project than I had at my "real" job. We shopped the prototype around to various game publishers and eventually convinced one to fully fund the development of another game idea I had.

That was all the opening I needed to quit my old job. Doing so meant I would take a substantial pay cut and have no benefits while at the same time support a family with two small kids and a mortgage in San Francisco. So, it was a huge risk. But the chance to work on something of my own creation and to be my own boss was too tempting to pass up. It's now two years later, we've had two games of our own design published (both being solid hits in the casual game market), are currently *working on games 3 and 4, and just gave ourselves a raise. So from my perspective, in hindsight, taking the plunge was worth the risk. The side benefits are I get to work at home in my jammies and have a super-flexible schedule that allows me to be involved in my kids' lives in ways I simply couldn't when I was working from 10 a.m. to 7 p.m. with a commute.*

What are the keys to success in your new career?

1. *Don't be afraid to take a risk. This is true not just of starting and maintaining a small company, but of designing original and successful games. Big game companies and their big games require such huge budgets that they can't afford to take many risks. As a small game maker making small games, you have the relative freedom to make something original that will stand out from the crowd.*

2. *Try not to spend money on anything that isn't going to directly benefit the business, but definitely spend what money you do have on things that raise the production value of the game you are making.*

3. *Keep design teams small. Three is a good number of designers for a casual game. Any more people than that becomes too many cooks in the kitchen. Make sure those three people are smart and have diverse backgrounds with skills and talents that complement each other.*

4. *Understand the audience and market for the games you want to make.*

5. *Test your game designs early and often with people who have never played your game before and are part of your target demographic. You will discover many, many problems with your "perfect" game design, and if you test early enough you will have time to fix those problems in order to make a better (and more successful) game.*

6. *Be able to do many things well. You don't have to be the best at anything, but in order to succeed you are going to have to wear many hats.*

7. *Create realistic schedules and try to never miss your milestones (at least through any fault of your own).*

8. *Communicate well with your teammates, your publishing partners, your contractors. Easier said than done, and few people are exceptionally good at it, but at least keep the lines of communication open.*

9. *Turn off your ego and then listen to your gut. Ninety percent of game design is common sense, while the other ten percent is inspiration. Huge egos will prevent inspired ideas from ever emerging and will destroy common sense in their large wakes.*

is also an online division for students who do not live near one of the campuses that provides a flexible option for earning your degree.

Readers who inhabit the southeast might be interested in the BFA in Computer Animation offered by Digital Media Arts College in Boca Raton, Florida. This is a three-year program that covers the storyboarding process, character modeling, character animation, filmmaking, advanced digital compositing, advanced applications in animation, and advanced visual effects. The college also offers a MFA in Special Effects Animation that covers high-end techniques such as motion capturing and other advanced techniques in animation in four semesters. Industry giants such as SEGA, Image-Works, and Disney are involved in this program at a college that is known for being technologically equipped. For those who reside in the southwest, Collins College in Tempe, Arizona, offers a bachelor's degree in Game Design that emphasizes designing, as well as writing supporting documentation for 2-D and 3-D games, including basic programming and working with 3-D animation applications. If you are not looking for a bachelor's degree, the Minnesota School of Business offers an Associate's degree in Programming and Game Development.

Essential Gear

Find your niche and stick to it. The video game industry has become so huge that most jobs are highly specialized unless the company is very small. Rather than possessing the skills, or having the opportunity, to work on all parts of a video game, the production process is more like the assembly of a movie, with each member of the crew (which can be over 50 people) performing their specific task without a sense of the final form the finished product will take. Rather than spreading yourself too thin, and seeming to lack a depth of skill at any one task, pick the aspect of game design at which you are best and learn it well.

Landmarks

If you are in your twenties . . . Do not be lulled into thinking that your expertise as a video game player will get you a job as a game designer. If you have spent your life immersed in video games since you could hold a joystick, you may think that all you need to put on your résumé is the number of hours you have spent playing with your Xbox or Play Station since toddlerhood. Think again. Read the sections in this chapter on the educational credentials and technical and design skills that you need, and acquire them before you start sending out résumés.

If you are in your thirties or forties . . . You are less likely than twenty-somethings to assume that video game playing skills will translate directly into video game designing skills. You have also probably had to unplug your games long enough to make a living for some years that you are willing to make some sacrifices to have a really fun job. Good. Take a shrewd look at your skills and experience and make the necessary augmentations to move into this new career in a realistic time frame.

If you are in your fifties . . . You are in an odd position age-wise, as potential employers will be expecting applicants in their twenties and thirties. Unfortunately, you are likely to face some age discrimination and you will have to prove that you have up-to-date technical skills and games market sensibilities to erase that skepticism.

If you are over sixty . . . If any profession has a generation gap, it is the games industry. If you are truly drawn to this career, you will need either fresh technical skills from a recent degree or a past career in a closely related field such as animation, graphic design, or computer programming.

Further Resources

The Game Institute is an online provider of education in video game design. Courses are not necessarily eligible for college credit, but this may not matter to you. They teach C++ programming for game development as well as 3-D graphics engine development.   http://www.gameinstitute.com

All Art Schools provides general information about entering the video game field, including interviews with designers for Xbox.   http://www.allartschools.com/faqs/gamedesigner-profile

Animation Arena lists information on video game design schools, with links.   http://www.animationarena.com/video-game-design.html

A Digital Dreamer.com features advice on how to enter high-tech graphic design careers such as video game design.   http://www.adigitaldreamer.com/articles/becomeavideogamedesigner.htm

Animator

Animator

Career Compasses

Get your bearings on what it takes to be a successful animator.

Relevant Knowledge of advanced animation techniques (60%)

Organizational Skills are useful because animation involves many tiny details (10%)

Communication Skills are crucial because animation takes collaborative teamwork (20%)

Ability to Manage Stress is an asset because animators must work to tight deadlines (10%)

Destination: Animator

If you are thinking of becoming an animator because you still enjoy watching cartoons as an adult, you are not alone. Animation is not just for children anymore. On the contrary, adult animation is a large and growing portion of the animation market. Television cartoons such as *The Simpsons, Family Guy, American Dad, King of the Hill,* and *South Park,* as well as feature films including *Fritz the Cat, Who Framed Roger Rabbit?, Cool World, Beavis and Butthead Do America,* and *Ultimate Avengers* are aimed almost exclusively at adult viewers. Colorful language, sexual content, or graphic violence are some features of animation targeted at adult audiences.

Children's cartoons are often violent, but in a bloodless way where the characters bounce back to life unharmed after being blown up, run over, or dropped off a cliff, to continue their quest to kill one another in the next episode. In fact, the tendency of children's cartoons to be extremely violent is spoofed in the *Itchy & Scratchy* cartoon-within-a-cartoon on *The Simpsons*. The difference in adult cartoons is that the violence is more realistic and gory, and characters can be maimed or killed. Japanese anime can be especially graphic in its violence. Sexual content or nudity is another distinguishing characteristic of adult animation, but it is less popular in the West than in Japan, where *hentai* (animated pornography) is big business. In the United States, language is the most frequent reason for animated work to be rated for adult audiences only.

Essential Gear

Prepare a sample reel. And make it good! Think of yourself as an actor preparing an audition tape for directors. The director will have to view many of them, and yours must jump out in order for you to get to the next stage of the interview process, let alone get the job. If you can create a portfolio of reels, even better. There is no set length but be aware that most potential employers are unlikely to watch beyond five minutes, whereas thirty seconds is probably not long enough to show them what you can do unless you put together a tape or DVD with numerous short reels to showcase your multifaceted talents. Include your best drawings in your portfolio, both hand-drawn and computer-generated.

Adult animation is not just animation that is unsuitable for children. Frequently, it simply contains references, vocabulary, and storylines that go above children's heads. In fact, cartoons aimed at children often contain jokes that are meant for the parents in the audience, such as pop-culture references and political satire. Of course, the uses for animation today go far beyond television series and films. Animation is used in video games (see Chapter 2 in this volume for more information on the related career of game designer), advertising, Web sites, and special effects.

Humans have been attempting to produce the perception of motion in drawings at least since the cave paintings of the paleolithic era. As a child, you probably played with (or even made) flipbooks, which represent another early attempt at animation. The advent of cinematography quickly led to the development of the first form of filmed animation, stop-motion.

The first widespread animation technique, called traditional or cel animation, involved photographing many drawings against a background. The drawings were traced (and later photocopied) onto transparent acetate sheets known as cels, colored, and photographed against a background, creating the illusion that the figures in the drawing were moving. The production of the cels was time-consuming, highly detailed work that involved a team of artists working together. By the beginning of the twenty-first century, the animation process became almost entirely computerized. Some drawings are still made by hand and scanned into computers, but most animators now work directly on the computer screen. Rotoscoping is a related animation technique where, instead of drawing freehand, artists trace live action source film. *A Scanner Darkly* (2006) is a recent example of rotoscoping.

Stop-motion animation did not disappear with the advent of cel animation; on the contrary, it remains popular today. Claymation, the manipulation and photographing of figures made from clay, has been used in *The Gumby Show*, *Wallace and Gromit*, and other television shows, films, and commercials. There are many other forms of stop-motion animation using real world objects such as paper cut-outs (see the first episode of *South Park* or *Monty Python's Flying Circus*), puppets (*The Nightmare Before Christmas* and *Robot Chicken*), or pixilation of live actors.

This overview does not even scratch the surface of the creative ways that artists have achieved the illusion of motion on film and in photographs. Additionally, the advent of computer animation has expanded animation techniques exponentially. The two basic distinctions are between 2-D and 3-D animation. Two-dimensional animation includes PowerPoint animation, Flash animation, and analog computer animation that is essentially computerized cel animation. *Sponge Bob Squarepants* is an example of 2-D animation. Three-dimensional animation involves manipulation of digital models by the animator, and it can be very realistic. The films *Toy Story* and *Shrek* are examples. Most modern special effects are also achieved with 3-D animation.

It is crucial for animators to continue their education and familiarize themselves with the latest techniques in digital animation. If that seems daunting, remember that creating animation is a team effort, and each member of the team brings a different skill set to the mix. Senior animators are supported by assistant animators, who work with background and layout artists, storyboard artists, visual development artists, graphic designers, and colleagues who specialize exclusively in special effects or specific animation techniques. With a little research, you can find out which job title suits your skills, interests, and talents.

You Are Here

You can begin your journey to animation from many different locales.

Do you have artistic talent? The computer does not help you decide what to draw, nor can a computer think of a compelling storyline, develop a character, or write clever dialogue. Computer skills are a necessary but not sufficient qualification for the job. If you have artistic talent, it probably manifested early in your childhood, in a love of drawing or sculpting or creating art in another medium. You may have buried this talent due to the demands of work and family, but now is the time to resurrect it.

Do you have advanced and relevant computer skills? This is the other side of the coin. Just as computer skills alone will not land you an animation job, neither will raw talent. Animation is primarily created on computers today and animators must know how to use digital drawing software. If you work in the field of 2-D animation, you will find a heavier reliance on old-fashioned pen-and-ink drawing ability, but 3-D animation involves more complex and industry-specific computer skills. At a minimum, you should be proficient in Photoshop, 3d Studio Max or a similar 3-D animation software package, Maya, and Lightware.

Can you go back to school? A career change into animation is likely to involve coursework in modern animation techniques, as well as aspects of cinematography, drawing, storytelling, editing, script writing, and related coursework. If you do not have the flexibility to take classes, or the interest in going back to school at this stage of your life, animation may not be a realistic career choice for you at present. You may not need to take any classes if you have closely related skills and experience, but if you were in that position you would probably not be reading this chapter.

Navigating the Terrain

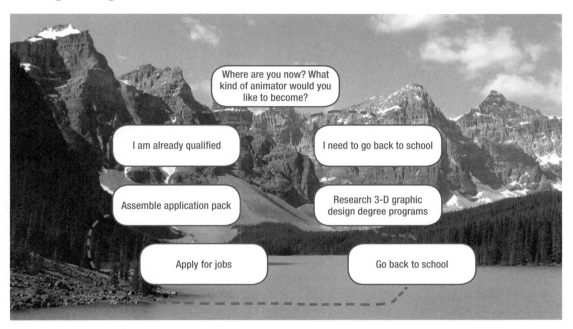

Where are you now? What kind of animator would you like to become?

I am already qualified

I need to go back to school

Assemble application pack

Research 3-D graphic design degree programs

Apply for jobs

Go back to school

Organizing Your Expedition

Before you set out, know where you are going.

Decide on a destination. Animators are usually either freelance artists or they work for a production company. Each type of working environment has its advantages and disadvantages. A freelancer has a great deal of flexibility, can work on a variety of animation projects, and can commute in slippers and jammies. The obvious downside is that you need to spend time marketing yourself to get work, and your income may not be stable, not to mention the lack of benefits. An animator at a production company may be working on a small piece of large project, have limited creative input, work in a corporate environment, and may long for more variety. Yet, the production company animator has a stable job with benefits, and may have more technological resources and bigger budgets for projects, which may reach a wider audience.

Stories from the Field

Trey Parker and Matt Stone
Creators of the *South Park* animated series
Denver, Colorado

Trey Parker and Matt Stone rose to (somewhat dubious) fame and fortune with the 1997 debut on the Comedy Central Network of their jointly conceived animated series *South Park*. Both animators grew up in the Denver suburbs, although Stone was born in Houston, Texas. Parker attended the University of Colorado but dropped out before graduating to pursue his career in animation, but Stone stayed to complete his degree in mathematics. Parker and Stone's first animated short, *Jesus vs. Frosty*, came out for the 1993 holiday season. They achieved some minor success with their next feature, *Cannibal! The Musical*, which was followed by *Jesus vs. Santa*. When they had the opportunity to create another animated short, they took the four boy characters from the *Jesus vs.* films and developed *South Park*, which was picked up by Comedy Central and aired 13 episodes in its debut season. Now in its thirteenth season on the network, *South Park* is an example of homemade, simplistic paper cut-out animation that evolved into one of the most successful and popular animated series ever.

Parker and Stone have not rested on their laurels but have been working on other projects simultaneous to growing the *South Park* franchise. As *South Park* grew, the series went beyond their initial animation and voice-over acting capabilities to involve a large cast and

Scout the terrain. As you read above, these days animation is used for many more purposes than feature-length animated films and television cartoons. Just because you do not live near Disney Studios does not mean that there are not interesting animation jobs in your own backyard. Animation is used to produce special effects in live action films, television shows and in advertising. Are any special effects companies located in your area? Are there Web design companies near you? Animation is frequently used in Web design today, and virtually every company, no matter what their business, has a Web site. What about local television stations? News programs need animators for some segments. Even the weather broadcast can be animated. Are there any video game production crew. Both Parker and Stone want to retain as much creative control over their work as possible. In 2000, when they created a Flash animation series about a Lhasa Apso dog called *Princess*, they did not allow anyone else to work with them. The series was destined for the Shockwave.com Web site, but was rejected as too obscene. The duo tried their hand at live action political satire with the short-lived *That's My Bush* in 2001. The per episode costs of production (about $700,000) proved prohibitively expensive and Comedy Central killed the series after one season. In addition to their television and film work, the pair also play in a band called DVDA. The band's songs have been used in their animated features, demonstrating that there seems to be no end to their creativity and energy.

Although neither Parker nor Stone appear to have ever held real jobs prior to launching their careers in animation, their career trajectory is instructive for anyone wishing to become an animator. They collaborated from the beginning, which is in keeping with the fact that animation is an inherently creative process that benefits from more ideas and input. Also, they did not have a lot of technical skills when they began, but they did have the discipline to bring their creative concepts to fruition with the tools at their disposal. Neither trained as an animator and sought a job in animation; rather, they created a finished product and shopped it to networks. This is another way into the industry, albeit one reliant on a certain amount of serendipity, timing, and old-fashioned good luck.

design companies nearby? Animators are certainly in demand in that field. Theme parks, casinos, and other entertainment venues can have animated displays. Is there one in your vicinity? Look around, and consider in what unexpected places you might find animation jobs.

Find the path that is right for you. Just as there are a variety of types of companies for which animators can work, and many different types of projects that involve animation, not to mention a vast array of technical tools for creating animation, there are also different job titles within the field of animation. Try on a few different hats to find the one that is right for you. You could be a modeler, a game designer, or a technical director, among numerous other options. Start scanning animation-related job ads today, and look at the qualifications and duties that go with different titles. After you have looked at a number of these listings, you will begin to ascertain what job title seems to be a good match for your talents, skills, and interests.

Essential Gear

Learn to draw. Yes, paper cut-outs, clay figures, and even live action are animated these days, but the heart and soul of the job is still drawing. Animators, unless they work only in a specific phase of production that involves working with drawings that have been done by other team members, spend hours drawing every day. In the old days, before computers, animators drew for eight or nine hours straight, even 15 to 20 hours if a deadline was near. You need to be able to draw cartoon characters, of course, and to develop a distinctive style of your own, but you must also know how to sketch, storyboard, and do life drawings and backgrounds.

Go back to school. Like game design and some other Internet and media careers in this volume, you will have to have the right educational credentials if you do not have extensive previous job experience in animation. The technical skills required are quite specific, but the good news is that there are many schools with flexible, part-time and online programs that will enable you to acquire them. Any course is going to cost you and before you lay down your tuition, consider whether the course can get you into the job you desire. Remember that learning the software is not enough. Animation has a technical side that you must understand thoroughly, but it is also an art form, and it requires creativity and non-technical skills like pacing, storytelling, character development, scene-building, and cinematography. A certificate in animation software is a necessary but not sufficient condition for obtaining an animation job. There a lot of schools offering certificates in animation techniques. Before you sign up with any of them, check out their success rates in placing graduates in the industry. Do not assume that the quality of instruction is similar at all of the schools in your area or online. Do some research and compare different institutions before registering for classes. Check out there refund policy and search for alumni in the business. Make sure that what they teach matches the qualifications sought in job ads for the positions you desire.

Landmarks

If you are in your twenties . . . Get cracking on your portfolio. Whether you are a student or working full time, use every spare minute to study computer animation software and start making your own animated shorts. When you have something to show for your efforts, start applying for jobs. Also look for internships that will enable you to get your foot in the door and learn on the job.

If you are in your thirties or forties . . . Do your research. You have been making your living somehow up to this point in a different field, and something about animation appeals to you for a career change. Zero in on what that is and develop it. Is it writing storylines and dialogue? Drawing characters? Do you have a cartoon series playing in your head? Do you like the technical challenges of special effects? Find your niche so you can focus your skill-building and job-hunting.

If you are in your fifties . . . You have the best chance of making a swift segue into the animation industry is you currently working in film, television, the comic industry, the arts, graphic design, or other related field. If you do not have related experience, ask yourself the questions posed in the advice above and start looking for schools.

If you are over sixty . . . You are in luck in that you should face limited job discrimination in this new career path. Especially if you work in one of the industries named above, your creativity, talent, and experience will be valued and respected. Just be certain that you are conversant with the latest technical terminology and that your computer skills are up to date.

Further Resources

Animation Mentor is an example of an online animation school. http://www.animationmentor.com
All Art Schools provides job preparation resources and educational information about careers in animation. http://www.allartschools.com/faqs/animation-schools.php

Animation Arena is a one-stop shop for animation information, including resources on 3-D and 2-D animation, Flash animation, animation schools, and more. http://www.animationarena.com

A Digital Dreamer.com will give you advice on various ways to enter the field of animation.   http://www.adigitaldreamer.com/articles/animation careerinfo.htm

E-Business Specialist

E-Business Specialist

Career Compasses

Get your bearings on what it takes to be a successful e-business specialist.

Relevant Knowledge of Internet software, as well as its application in your industry (30%)

Organizational Skills are always an asset in any field, and the corporate world is no exception (20%)

Communication Skills are important because you will be working as part of a team and participating in many meetings (30%)

Ability to Manage Stress is useful because most corporate jobs today face frequent "reorganization" (20%)

Destination: E-Business Specialist

The term "e-business," short for "electronic business," is the standard name for business conducted on the Internet, generally via the World Wide Web, and sometimes over e-mail. It logically follows that an "e-business specialist" is someone who helps companies conduct business on the Internet. The good news is that the term is used broadly to cover professionals in every aspect of business management, including human resources, all levels and divisions of business management and administration, sales and marketing, labor relations, international business, inventory and purchasing, and so on. This means that, whatever your current area of business specialization, you can apply it to e-business. There are some Internet-specific business considerations with which you will need to become familiar, such as Web and e-mail marketing strategies, but the transition from brick-and-mortar business to online business is likely to be a smooth one regardless of your previous experience.

E-business specialists are subdivided into two types of roles: technological and non-technological. The former are sometimes referred to as "e-business IT specialists." These e-business professionals focus on the technical aspects of running a business online rather than the traditional business side. The background and education of an e-business IT specialist must be in computer science, with strong programming and Web development skills. E-business and e-business IT specialists work together to run a successful online business. Each skill set complements the other, and neither could manage an online business without the other. That being said, one important caveat to note here is that the division of labor is dependent upon the size of the company. As a general rule, the larger the company, the smaller and more specific will be each job function, with the inverse of that true for smaller companies. In really tiny e-businesses, one person may attempt to perform all roles, or delegate only certain duties (such as programming of the Web site or marketing it) that are beyond their technical expertise or business acumen.

Essential Gear

Be a show-off. Put yourself in the position of the person interviewing you: What would convince you to hire you? As you prepare your résumé and cover letter, write down a list of your best business and technical skills. Can you quantify them by pointing to specific gains for past employers? If you increased regional sales by 15 percent after introducing an e-marketing campaign, make that the centerpiece of your cover letter. If you designed a database that made it twice as fast for your distributors to check and replenish inventory, talk it up in your interview.

As you contemplate this career change, consider what business and technical skills you bring from your previous education and experience. Do you have broad but shallow skills in many aspects of business management? Are you a techie with great computer skills but no idea how to run a business? Or do you have in-depth knowledge of one business specialty, such as sales? When you look at job advertisements, pay careful attention to the size of the company and the breadth of skills that are being sought. There is enough variety that you should be able to find a good match for your skills and interests.

Broadly speaking, an e-business specialist manages the online presence of a given company. This can include informational Web sites that do not directly sell the company's products or services but form an important part of the company's public relations strategy, e-commerce Web sites that sell direct to consumers, e-commerce Web sites that sell business-to-business, and internal company Web sites that provide information and training to employees. The e-business specialist must coordinate and integrate the company's Web sites with its sales and marketing campaigns, keeping the company's branding consistent, and the Web site content current. Applications and functionality must be state-of-the-art in an environment where technology evolves quickly and user expectations change at a fast pace. Although an e-business specialist works with Web development staff to design, implement, and administer a company's Web portfolio, a fairly high level of technical knowledge is expected of most e-business specialists due to the nature of the medium in which they work. In order to strategize how a company can most effectively leverage the power of the Internet for sales, business development or employee relations, the e-business specialist must be comfortable and familiar with this new business medium.

Essential Gear

Learn the lingo. Both the corporate world and the tech crowd speak in their own idiom, with acronyms, technical jargon, and syntax that is not found in standard English. Becoming conversant with this lingo will help you to bond with potential coworkers in your interviews, and will serve as a reassurance to potential employers that you know what you are talking about. Think of it this way: If the Wiki set considers themselves clever and funny for calling their language "Markdown," so do you.

An e-business IT specialist, sometimes called e-business technology specialist, must integrate various Web technologies needed to run an Internet-based business, or section of a business. Skills needed include programming, fluency with graphics software, database integration, and can include network administration in some environments. The IT specialist will be expected to solve technical problems, develop and test proprietary software, and implement the designs and functionality desired by the business development side of the company. The tech and non-tech e-business professionals must work closely together to implement a consistent vision for the company's Web portfolio that achieves the goals set for it. The IT side of the team must tell the business side what is technically feasible and both tech and non-tech e-business specialists need superb project management skills.

It is important to keep in mind that e-business is a rapidly changing environment. A decade ago, some writing, editing and Dreamweaver skills might have gotten you a job maintaining a company's internal Web site and a title of e-business IT manager. Now, employers are expecting a skill set from one employee that straddles Web site design, Web marketing, Web development, and even logistics, sales, and marketing. That breadth of expectation may sound rather daunting, but there are some areas of e-business in which you can specialize, and there are jobs available in which you can stick pretty closely to your niche. If you have strong Web programming skills you could be a Web developer. In this role you would design as well as implement and maintain both Internet and Intranet Web sites and proprietary applications. If you have a head for statistics, you might consider a career as an e-business analyst, also known as a Web analyst. In this job you would track and analyze metrics related to the Web site activities of your company or industry. Another option is to go into e-business consulting. In this capacity, you would help clients to leverage the power of technology to pursue their business needs and goals, and implement corporate initiatives. Many companies today wish to harness technology to improve efficiency and to develop the full potential of e-commerce for their business. An e-business consultant has to be skilled at going into a new office environment and quickly developing an understanding of the nature of the business, the work practices and style, and the ways in which technological solutions have succeeded or failed in that particular industry in the past. The consultant analyzes problems, conducts research, makes recommendations, and develops e-business solutions and strategies in consultation with the internal executives. The end product may be a written or oral report and, in many cases, the e-business consultant will stay to implement the preferred solutions and to assist the client company with change-management. Read on to help you determine which area of e-business specialization is right for you.

You Are Here

You can begin your journey to e-business from many different locales.

Do you have Internet-related business experience? When a potential employer is evaluating your fitness for a job, their primary consideration is what added value you bring to their workforce. If you have conventional business experience but little experience in the world of e-commerce, well, that is exactly their problem. E-business is a relatively new area for most brick-and-mortar companies. What they are looking for in an e-business specialist is someone who can tell them something they do not already know. They want experience, Internet-related technical skills, and a track record of success.

Do you have Web-related technical skills? E-business is the fusion of good old-fashioned sales and marketing with the technological opportunities created by the Internet. If you cannot get into this field via your

Navigating the Terrain

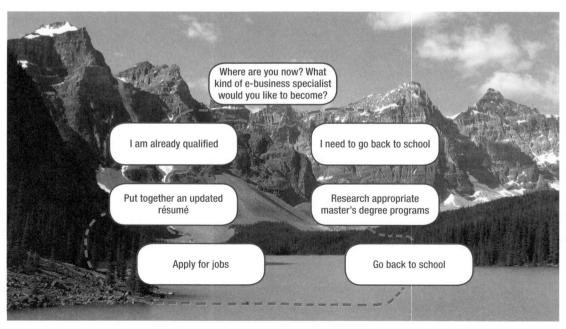

Where are you now? What kind of e-business specialist would you like to become?

I am already qualified

I need to go back to school

Put together an updated résumé

Research appropriate master's degree programs

Apply for jobs

Go back to school

business savvy, you can get into it via your IT skills. A background in any Web-related field, whether in design, graphics, networks, databases, or other computer programming skills, will help you to find a good fit with the right employer. Just be certain that your software and programming language knowledge is up-to-date.

Do you have project management experience? The work necessary to support business functions on the Internet, whether for internal, business-to-business or business-to-consumer applications, takes teams of employees with different job titles and skill sets. At mid-career and higher levels, an e-business specialist functions as a project manager to integrate all phases of e-business plans with the various employees needed to design, implement, test, maintain, and update e-commerce applications. Project management experience, even in another field, is going to be a valuable asset as you make this career change.

Organizing Your Expedition

Before you set out, know where you are going.

Decide on a destination. The broad category of e-business specialist encompasses several different types of professional roles. Your first fork in the road on your journey to e-business will require you to pick a technical or non-technical area of e-business in which to focus your job search. This decision will largely be made for you based upon your previous education and professional experience. The modern business world is divided fairly rigidly between techies and non-techies, and you know which one you are. The line blurs slightly in the e-business sector since everyone involved must have some technical knowledge, but there is still a demarcation between those who are making the business decisions and those who are doing the coding and site administration.

Once you have decided whether you are an aspiring e-business specialist or e-business IT specialist, you can further parse out your job prospects by choosing an area of focus within those broad categories. Sales, marketing, logistics, research and analysis, and project management are possible non-techie options. Again, let your previous experience, interests, and skills be your guide. Specializations on the IT side include, but are not limited

Notes from the Field

Monica Kelley
E-Business IT specialist
New York, New York

What were you doing before you decided to change careers, and why did you change your career?

I worked for an Internet start-up. Actually, it was the American office of a Tokyo-based Web design company. When the dotcom bubble burst in the summer of 2000, the home office decided to pull the plug on their New York outpost. Jobs in the technology field were suddenly scarce as everyone and their dog got laid off at the same time. After tasting the excitement, freedom, and perks of working for an informal start-up, I was reluctant to go back to the staid corporate world, but I also knew that I needed the stability of a big company where IT was just one small part of a larger, more solvent whole.

How did you make the transition?

I scoured the job ads in the *New York Times* for months. It took me four months to find a job. I wasn't married to staying in the tech industry,

to, Web design and development, network administration, programming, software development, and software testing. Depending upon your background, there may be other niches that you could fill. If you have a law degree, for example, you might consider the growing field of e-business law. If you have a finance or economics degree, you will find those skill sets in demand in certain contexts. If you have a background in information or resource management, this is also easily applicable to the online business universe. Heck, even if you studied anthropology you can set yourself up as an expert in cyberculture. The e-workscape is continuously changing and you can basically make up your own specialty at this point.

Scout the terrain. Unfortunately, the fact that you will be working in an online environment, where you may spend your days communicating with clients or facilitating communication with customers around *but prior to the startup I had worked on the launch of one of the first Internet home banking services, so I figured I had to stay with where my experience lay to have any hope of being hired. The job I ended up getting was with an insurance company. The job required a master's but they didn't specify in what field. Obviously, they were thinking MBA, but my MPA was close enough. I really talked up my appropriateness for the position in the interview.*

What are the keys to success in your new career?

I'd say the hardest part is playing the corporate game. Everything is done in teams, and there are endless meetings. By the time you have started one project, the high-ups have changed the plan and you need to hold more meetings and switch gears. Creativity and individuality are not always encouraged or rewarded. It can be a dull job. I guess my best advice is: Don't lose sight of the big picture. You work to live, not the other way around, and any job you can get that pays the bills is a good job in this economy.

the world, does not mean that you can telecommute as an e-business specialist. The team nature of the work, coupled with the need to make e-business solutions specific to an individual company's culture, require that most e-business specialists work in the physical offices of their employer. This means that you need to find out what jobs are in your area by looking at local listings or you need to consider if you are willing to move, and where, for the right job.

Find the path that is right for you. If nothing else this chapter should give you confidence that, whatever your educational and professional background, you can draw on it to move into the dynamic e-business sector. Depending upon your qualifications, it may take some time, and you may have to take a course or move through a few positions to find the best fit, but you can get there with a little research and persistence.

Go back to school. Once upon a time (in Internet parlance, that means about a decade ago), e-business duties were undertaken by managers and executives whose educations and work experience had not prepared them for the opportunities and challenges of the Internet. At that time, the price of entry for an entry-level e-business job was the same as any other business job: a bachelor's degree in business or marketing or a related field, and the ticket to an e-business managerial position was an MBA. Fast-forward to today, when schools have established programs specifically in e-business. To a large extent, they have taken the traditional business curriculum and put an "e-" in front of every course, so that you can now study e-marketing and e-management to specifically prepare you for an e-business job. Many of these courses are offered through two-year associates degree programs. They are ubiquitous, so you should not have a problem finding one in your area. Do you need to take one? It depends. Start by looking at job advertisements for positions that interest you, and conduct some informational interviews. You should quickly get a sense if prospective employers see your existing background and education as e-appropriate or not.

Landmarks

If you are in your twenties . . . Get an "e-something" degree. At your age, prospective employers will see you as part of an Internet-savvy generation that has grown up online. They will expect strong technical skills as a matter of course, and will want to see that you have geared your education towards an e-business job.

If you are in your thirties or forties . . . You fall into a gray-area, age-wise, where some employers will value traditional brick-and-mortar business degrees, skills, and experience, and others will expect you to be e-savvy. Play it by ear and try your luck on the job market before investing in a course, but do not wait too long to augment your skills if the employers do not hear you singing their tune.

If you are in your fifties . . . You will have to prove, via previous professional successes, that your business skills are useful in the online business environment. If you have held, say, a brick-and-mortar sales job, at which you were successful, and you would like to try your hand at e-sales, you will need to prove to prospective employers that you know something about the online sales environment. You have probably achieved some stature in your career by this stage, so it may be humbling to be in a position to prove your worth. Suck it up and you may land your dream job.

If you are over sixty . . . You are going to be considered part of the generation of brick-and-mortar business managers who need to be dragged kicking and screaming into the information age. You will have to be twice as tech-savvy as a younger applicant to be considered for the job. Your best bet is to target your search to companies that are looking for strong general business skills that can be applied to an online environment. This may mean focusing on larger companies where positions are more defined and a separate technical staff exists to implement the ideas of the business management staff.

Further Resources

CIO Index functions like a news-filter site with e-business and other IT governance and strategy articles. Contains forums for discussion and lengthy archives. http://www.cioindex.com/articles/index.php/category/estrategy

CIO.com contains the latest e-business news. Also has job postings. http://www.cio.com/topic/5693/E_Business

Entrepreneur.com offers advice on how to start an online business. http://www.entrepreneur.com/ebusiness/index.html

Tech Republic provides resources and advice for e-business. http://search.techrepublic.com.com/search/e-business.html

Webmaster

Webmaster

Career Compasses

Get your bearings on what it takes to be a successful webmaster.

Relevant Knowledge of Web design, as well as project management skills (40%)

Organizational Skills are key to a happy team and projects completed on time (10%)

Communication Skills are useful if you are working with a team and crucial for dealing with clients (30%)

Ability to Manage Stress is important because you face deadlines and unforeseen technical problems on the way to meeting them (20%)

Destination: Webmaster

The first step in the process of deciding whether webmaster is the career for you is distinguishing what, exactly, a webmaster does. A webmaster is the person who has overall authority over the design and programming of a Web site. He or she is responsible for both the functionality and performance of the Web site, which may mean running it day-to-day. This is different from a Web designer, who may not maintain the site after his or her design role is completed. It is also different from an e-business specialist, whose primary concern is sales, marketing, and other business aspects of a Web site. Likewise, a Web entrepreneur is someone who owns a Web-based business and focuses on the business end. He or she may have the technical ability to run a Web site, but more than likely hires other Web designers, webmasters, and IT and business staff. Web producers can easily be confused with Web masters since the job titles are frequently used interchangeably in job advertisements. The main distinction is that the Web producer is more of a project manager, in charge of the overall results of the efforts of the designers, programmers, and e-business specialists from the concept to the completion of the Web site.

At this stage a webmaster might take over to maintain the site and assume responsibility for its functionality and performance. Bear in mind, though, as you conduct your job search, that many advertisements will be headlined, "Webmaster/Web Producer." Take that as a cue that you will be working with a project team, and you will be responsible for a site from its conception through its design and build phases and beyond.

Essential Gear

Get a book. Yes, you have this book, and that is a very good start. But the coverage of each career option in this volume is, out of necessity, broad rather than deep. It is designed to give you basic information about careers that might interest you so that you can make an initial assessment of their suitability, and point you in the direction of further resources to pursue your career goals. If your plans now include becoming a webmaster, you will want to read one of the many books on the market today that are devoted exclusively to this career choice. Here are three to get you started: *Teach Yourself How To Become a Webmaster* by James L. Mohler, *Webmastering for Dummies* by Daniel A. Tauber, and *Webmaster in a Nutshell* by Stephen Spainhour. You will also need a separate book just on HTML, and probably one for each programming language or software program that you use.

Another job title you might encounter is "Web developer." This is yet another name for webmaster, and this title is used when the webmaster is primarily responsible for the programming of the site. A Web developer may or may not participate in the site's design, but he or she definitely does the scripting/programming and will be expected to have extensive and cutting edge technical skills. You may encounter job advertisements that state "Webmaster/Web Developer," and you can interpret those to mean that a high standard of technical knowledge is required. As you can see, there is no standardization of job titles so you have to read each advertisement carefully, and look under a variety of headings, to find the position you seek.

At the lowest level, a webmaster may be tasked with little more than reading site feedback, fixing bad links, and updating content that is provided by others. At the other extreme, a webmaster is a jack-of-all-Web-trades who oversees the entire Web site the way a CEO oversees an entire company. Everything to do with the site is done by one person. This last view of the role is somewhat outdated. A decade ago, when you could hand code an entire Web site in plain HTML using the Microsoft Word application Notepad, the position could be filled by one person, who could reasonably be expected to master the requisite skill set. Today, Web sites are so complex and the technical and business knowledge needed to build them so immense and varied, that it is virtually impossible for one person to do it all. As a general rule, the more a company relies on its Web site for revenue, the more resources they will devote to it. This means that a webmaster working solo is probably maintaining his or her own site, or the site of an enterprise that maintains a minimal Web presence and does not want to devote many resources to Web development.

So where does that leave you, the aspiring webmaster? Well, think of this ambiguity as an advantage: Whatever your level of technical expertise, there is probably a webmaster job at your level. And you can breathe a sigh of relief that you do not have to study the daunting array of design, scripting, and programming options that exist in order to make this career change. In a middle-of-the-road interpretation of the role that is probably most appropriate to today's IT workplace, the webmaster is the single point of contact for the Web site. This webmaster handles technical queries either single-handedly or forwards them to the appropriate Web development team member. Anything related to the site's content falls under the purview of the client or the business side of the management team. This role is administrative in part and hands-on technical in part, depending upon the size of the company. This level of webmaster must know all about hosting, budgets, Web design, and have enough technical knowledge to maintain most functions of the site even if they oversee some specialists who handle specific technical aspects of its functionality.

You Are Here

You can begin your journey to webmaster from many different locales.

Are you fluent in HTML? How about XHTML, XML, CSS, PHP, CGI/Perl, HTTP, JavaScript, MySQL, Apache server configuration, Linux, Unix, Shockwave? For a webmaster, HTML, which is the basic language of all Web pages, is only the first in a long list of technical skills to learn. In some other IT jobs, you can have one area of specialization, such as Oracle databases, and stick with it, but a webmaster must have a broad skill set. Think of it this way: Rather than being completely fluent in French and only French, you need to be conversant in French, Italian, German, Russian, Japanese, Portuguese, Spanish, Swedish, Danish, and Hindi, with a fair command of Tagalog and Hungarian expected. You do not need to be an expert in every programming language and software program on the market, but your command cannot be too shallow either.

Have you done technical writing? It is not a requirement but, rather, a common background that webmasters frequently have. Technical writing is a job in the tech industry that is accessible to people with a non-technological background. At the height of the dot-com boom, everyone wanted a piece of the Internet action, even if their undergraduate degree was in linguistics, not computer science. Technical writers could segue into writing for the Web without much difficulty. As the industry has matured, it has become tougher to get jobs without a more solid background and education in the field.

Do you have friends in online places? A funny thing about being a webmaster: you need a Web site on which to exercise your masterful skills and talents. If you are a new or aspiring webmaster, companies and individuals who depend upon their Web sites for their business may be hesitant to put a newbie in charge. This is where connections come in. To build your portfolio, you can offer to work on Web sites for people and businesses that you know well. Another option is to make the acquaintance of the Web team at your current employer and offer to help them. Demonstrate your willingness to do small jobs like checking for and fixing bad links. If you can get your foot in the door there, you might be able to change careers without changing employers.

Navigating the Terrain

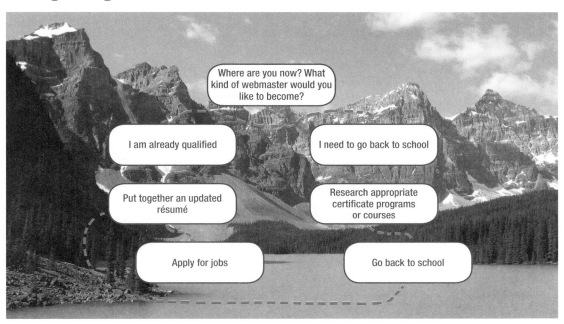

Organizing Your Expedition

Before you set out, know where you are going.

Decide on a destination. Webmasters work either as freelancers or as part of a corporate information technology (IT) group. Your work environment and job duties will vary considerably between those two situations. Freelancers sometimes work on-site, but most often work from home. If you desire or need to telecommute, freelancing might be the right path for you to follow. If you prefer the stability, benefits, and support of a larger team environment, you may prefer to look for a job in an IT group. Larger companies will have an in-house IT department, whereas smaller ones may farm this work out to freelancers or stand-alone Web design companies—a third employment environment to consider.

Scout the terrain. Because webmasters use a variety of technical and design skills, and may either work in teams or solo, you have quite a few

Notes from the Field

Gary Poole
Senior Web developer
Chattanooga, Tennessee

What were you doing before you decided to change careers?

I worked as a radio talk show host for a prominent local station.

Why did you change your career?

Oh, the usual reason: [The] station was sold and budget cuts took out half of the employees. The corporate homogenization of radio made it no longer viable as a career.

How did you make the transition?

I looked at what other skills I had outside of broadcasting, and since I had learned Web development over the years (supplementing my radio

options for how you enter the profession. The choice you make depends upon local opportunities, so start looking at job ads. It is also contingent upon your current level of technical skills. If you do not yet possess the full range of typical webmaster skills, look for openings for technical writers, tech support personnel, or spots on the Web development team that mesh with your current abilities. If you are coming from a graphic design background, look for Web-related graphics jobs that can get your foot in the door as you build your programming skills. If freelancing is your goal, print some business cards and advertise for clients.

Find the path that is right for you. If you are not sure whether you want to be a freelance webmaster, a member of a corporate IT group, or employee of a stand-alone Web design company, talk to people in each of these roles to ask them questions about their working life. Call or e-mail local webmasters to schedule informational interviews. Whilst you are finding out if their work situation is appropriate for you, you can also show them your résumé and portfolio and see if you have the right qualifications for each environment. This way you will both learn more about the position you desire and find out what you need to do to get it.

salary with custom design work), I decided to see if I could get employ-ment in that field. Which I did very quickly.

What are the keys to success in your new career?

Understanding the specific needs of both the client and the intended audience for the Web site. The company I work for specializes in Web development for small businesses and churches, two markets that are often overlooked by the larger design firms. We work hand-in-hand with each client figuring exactly what they need—and more impor-tantly, what they don't need—and how to tailor it to attract the type of customers they are looking for. Being able to communicate with people and understand their needs and wants is absolutely vital.

Go back to school. There are no specific degree requirements for web-masters. Instead, there are specific technical and design skills that you must demonstrate. A degree, certificate, or other claim of proficiency is not going to convince potential employers that you can run their Web site. The only thing they care to see is your portfolio—proof that you know what you are doing. Since the job of webmaster combines both pro-gramming and graphic design, as well as writing, there are a lot of skills to master. Put yourself in a potential employer's shoes: What would you need to know to trust that the person you are interviewing could do the job? The proof is not a B.S. in computer science; it is in your portfolio. That said, most job advertisements will list educational requirements, and get-ting to the interview stage will be easier if you are qualified on paper. You can bolster your academic qualifications in two ways: One, you can go back to school for a B.S. or M.S. degree in computer science; two, you can take individual courses in various programming languages, such as C, and other Web development tools, such as Active X, Internet servers, object standards, image maps, HTML, network administration, electronic money transactions, e-commerce engineering, service-provider interac-tion, Web branding, and the latest scripting languages as they evolve.

Landmarks

If you are in your twenties . . . Stay in school. Seriously, focus on the educational requirements of webmasters first. A decade ago, skills and experience were enough to get you a job because most webmaster skills were not taught in schools. Now, such classes are everywhere, and someone young enough to have attended school since their advent will be expected by potential employers to have taken them.

Essential Gear

Put together a portfolio. This chapter has failed if it has not driven home the point that potential employers will want to see evidence of your skills. Your qualifications on paper may get you in the door for an interview, but you will not be hired unless the powers that be are impressed with Web sites that you have designed and coded yourself. If you do nothing else to prepare for this career transition, put together an online portfolio of which you are proud.

If you are in your thirties or forties . . . You are possibly old enough that employers will be looking more for experience than education on your résumé, but do not count on it. Before you leave your current job, sign up for some evening and weekend Web development and management courses. Do that in addition and simultaneous to building your portfolio.

If you are in your fifties . . . You might as well face your biggest problem head on: age discrimination. You are of the generation of worker who was put in the position of adapting your business practices to the information age, the generation that hired young, Web-savvy workers to build Web sites and drag you and your company kicking and screaming into the digital age. If you want potential employers to see you as an Internet superstar, you are going to have to work doubly hard to convince them that you are a technical expert.

If you are over sixty . . . Read the advice for fifty-somethings and then resolve to work twice as hard as them to show potential employers that you are on the bleeding edge of technological expertise and Web design trends. Use any connections you have built up over your career to move into the Web side of your current business or to build clientele as a freelancer.

Further Resources

Big Webmaster features a variety of resources for webmasters, including online tutorials for most common scripts and programs. http://www.bigwebmaster.com

Webmaster Toolkit contains SEO tools, Web utilities, domain tools, HTML tools, and more. http://www.Webmaster-toolkit.com

Walshaw.com provides webmaster resources including a collection of tools and articles. Most services are free. http://www.walshaw.com

Boogie Jack.com contains HTML and CSS tutorials among other webmaster resources. http://www.boogiejack.com

Web Designer

Web Designer

Career Compasses

Get your bearings on what it takes to be a successful Web designer.

Relevant Knowledge of the technical and design tools needed to build a Web site (50%)

Organizational Skills to produce Web sites on time and to order (20%)

Communication Skills to negotiate with your clients effectively (20%)

Ability to Manage Stress is key to dealing with demands from clients and deadlines (10%)

Destination: Web Designer

Who doesn't have a Web site today? Even your dog and cat have a Web site. Can hamster.com be far behind? Maybe you could get the job designing it. Hey, why not? For every Web site in existence, someone got an idea, registered and paid for the domain name, wrote the content, chose the graphics, decided on the functionality and navigation, and coded it. There are a lot of WYSIWYG (what you see is what you get) software programs that enable people with limited computer skills to set up basic

Web sites, and even set-up fairly sophisticated e-commerce sites for their businesses. Yet, there is still, and for the foreseeable future will be, a demand for professional Web designers and programmers who can create more complex and individualized Web sites.

Opportunities in Web design range widely depending upon your interests, skills and location. In fact, the field is so broad that Web designers usually specialize. The main distinction is between those with an eye for design who focus on the visual aspects of a site—the look and feel—and those stereotypical "geeks" who are involved with the back-end technical side, that is, coding the HTML and other languages used to bring the designeris vision to life. Within these two general areas, the work is further subdivided. There are some Web designers who specialize in creating banner ads, and that is all they do. Others make Flash movies for site intros, and other sophisticated audio-visual effects. On the technical side, one could gravitate towards e-commerce and tinker with the programming of shopping carts and other facets of online selling. Web designers can be self-employed freelancers, who provide full-service Web design services out of their home and procure their own clients. A Web designer can also work for a Web design company as part of a Web production team, or work as in-house Web support staff for a company. Most businesses today consider at least a basic Web site to be a necessity for marketing purposes, even if they do not use it for e-commerce. Disseminating information online is considered essential today for all media outlets, academic institutions, and governments. Not only do new entities need to set up Web sites, but Web trends and technologies change so fast that existing sites continually need to be updated to give them a fresh look and new functionality. Advertising

Essential Gear

Chart a course for the future. To say that Web design technology changes rapidly is to understate the situation. By the time you have finished reading this paragraph, several new technologies, and new iterations of existing technologies, will have appeared on the Web design scene. Make it your business to keep track of emerging trends (e.g., we are surfing the Web from phones and other handheld devices now—what medium will be next?) and update your technical skills continually. In addition to the technical side, preferences for the look, feel, and navigation of Web sites also evolves. Make sure your designs not only have the latest technical bells and whistles, but look current, too.

agencies and marketing and PR consulting firms increasingly rely on the Web as an important medium for representing their clients, so potential Web designers with a background in these fields may not have to move further than down the hall.

The outlook for this career path is bright, but the barriers to entry are high. With computer skills becoming as basic to each new generation as reading and writing used to be, you need to have quite sophisticated technical and design skills to get paid for Web design. A Web designer needs to know all of the commonly used programming languages, and he or she must keep learning new ones as they come out. No field in the technology sector is static, and Web design technology evolves faster than most. Even the simplest Web site involves multiple Web technologies such as HTML, XML, Javascript, CSS, and more. New iterations of existing technologies are released continually, and new technologies are being developed as you read this chapter. People are also browsing the Word Wide Web on an increasing variety of devices besides computers. The new technology needed to design Web sites that can be accessed from these devices creates more opportunities for specialization.

Although a Web designer will likely concentrate advanced skill development in one aspect of Web site design and programming, there are certain basic skills that are common to all. Someone looking to move into the field of Web design should start by learning basic Hypertext Markup Language (HTML), the fundamental coding language for the Web. Sure, all those WYSIWYG programs can code for you, but if you want to be a professional Web designer, you need to know how to write code, fix code, and generally make code do more tricks than you can find in Dreamweaver, FrontPage, GoLive, and the other HTML editors. The Word Wide Web Consortium (see link at the end of this chapter) is always busy updating HTML. The current version is HTML 5, but that could change by the time this book gets into your hands. A related language is eXtensible Markup Language (XML), which helps you control data that are linked to a Web page. Once you can throw up some basic text on a Web page, the next step is to add some graphics. A Web designer should be comfortable manipulating .jpeg and .gif files in Photoshop, at a minimum, and other graphics editing software. Today, most Web site owners expect the graphics on their Web site to move. The most commonly used software for animation is Macromedia's Flash. Pack this program in your suitcase of skills, and then move onto sound, adding streaming audio files with

Real Play and Real Audio or embedding MIME files in your HTML. This is only the tip of the Web design iceberg. Next, you will want to learn how to add Cascading Style Sheets (CSS) to your HTML to give you much more control over the appearance of your Web sites. JavaScript, and its cousin, Ajax, are languages that are usually used along with CSS to make Web pages more dynamic, in keeping with contemporary expectations for their navigation capabilities. When you click on a selection from a drop-down menu on a Web page that opens up a window with a new page, that is usually done with JavaScript, and such functionality is considered basic today. Those are the basics that any Web designer should know, but each area of specialization will have its own languages and technologies.

While almost anyone can learn to be a Web designer, there are certain educational and career backgrounds that will make the transition easier. Those with a background in engineering and mathematics are well-placed to have an easier time with the programming side, and intrepid Web explorers with a background in any aspect of design, from graphic to interior, should find it a stimulating challenge to apply their talents to Web design. Since the Web is used to sell, sell, sell, a background in sales or marketing could be an asset. If you cannot find a way to connect your previous education or employment background to Web design, do not worry. Some of the best Web designers were simply individuals who put in the time and effort to acquire the necessary skills.

You Are Here

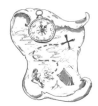

You can begin your journey to being a Web designer from many different locales.

Do you have an online portfolio? Before anyone hires you as a Web Designer, they are going to want to see sites that you have designed previously. This means that prior to landing your first paying gig, you are going to have to make a lot of Web sites. Some of these can be samples designed just for your portfolio, but others should be real sites, done for anyone you can persuade to let you work for free. As you gain more experience, the process will go faster and you will start to get paying gigs, but those first, free sites are going to hurt.

Do you have a related degree or work experience? A degree in computer science or graphic design will open doors, but it is not the only key. Virtually any experience in visual arts, marketing, advertising, or selling can be applied to Web design, as can some skills in the hard sciences and mathematics. Web designers often specialize as the field is too large, and the technologies too numerous, to do everything well. Let your past be your guide to a viable area of specialization in your new career.

Do you like staring at a computer screen for many hours each day? Don't laugh: This is a valid consideration! Many jobs require significant computer use, and sitting at a desk all day, often in a windowless cubicle, is often cited by career changers as a reason for seeking new horizons. As a Web designer, your work—all of it, 100 percent—will be done sitting at a computer, typing in fiddly bits of code or getting that graphic in just the right spot or making sure clicking on each button leads to the right page on the site. It is detail-oriented work, and, barring a strong wireless connection, not work that can really be done outside in the sunshine. Just because

Navigating the Terrain

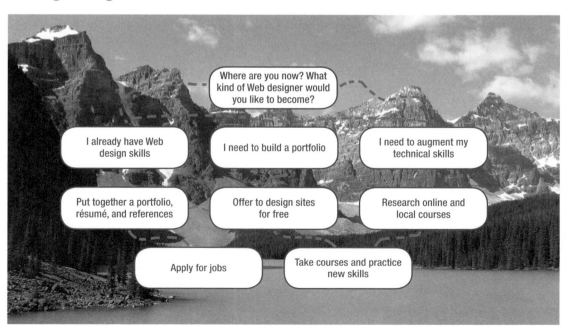

Notes from the Field

Joe Peacock
Web designer
Atlanta, Georgia

What were you doing before you decided to change careers?

The day before I took my first job as a paid Web designer, I was selling *Andy Griffith* and *I Love Lucy* collectibles at the mall by day and assisting the night owls in the computer lab at my school at night. Then someone saw a goofy Web site I did about Henry Rollins vs. Batman (this was 1996, and to see images on a Web site was still considered "cutting edge"). Obviously, I was an expert in Web design for being able to do this and I did nothing to dissuade my new boss from believing as such.

Why did you change your career?

Well, I sold crappy commemorative plates in the mall and helped people print their term papers for nearly 18 hours a day combined. I think I would have taken a job sewing the buttons back on the Chippendale's models' ripped-off shirts by that point, but this came to me first.

How did you make the transition?

By reading . . . A lot. I had an understanding of how HTML worked, and back then, no one really had any concepts about how a Web-

you enjoyed designing a site or two does not mean that you will necessarily enjoy doing so all day, every day. It is something to think about. Some people who turn hobbies into careers feel like they never work a day in their life, but others lose sight of what drew them to the field in the first place.

Organizing your Expedition

Before you set out, know where you are going.

Decide on a destination. There are many forks in the road to becoming a Web designer. The direction you take at each junction will determine your final destination. So, consider the following questions as you map your route: Do you want to work for a Web design company or freelance?

based application would look or work, or the idea of ad campaigns or marketing their business on the Web. As people started figuring it out, those of us who were not college professors or researchers and were using the net for this new marketing/e-commerce initiative pretty much had to figure out how magazine designers, billboard designers, retail shelf/rack designers, and shipping companies all did what they did, so we could translate all of it into "click here to buy." We were all clueless back then.

What are the keys to success in your new career?

Meeting new people, reading new things . . . Constantly checking in on how other designers are doing what they do and figuring out what you find great about it and what you dislike about it. You pick up the good habits, try to avoid the bad ones. Keeping up on how people interact with all things—not just the Web—is a massive component to making things people like using. Lastly, keeping an eye on people and things as you shop and visit places is a huge aspect—note the colors, trends, styles, architecture of spaces . . . When you go to design a sports-based site, there are very key components to the concept of "sports" in the modern era that go well beyond grass and goalposts, and knowing what people are experiencing (not just seeing) when they watch football or hockey on TV and in person is vital.

The path to these two destinations diverges at a crucial point: As a company employee, you will work on sites for clients that the sales and marketing division of your corporation brings in; as a freelancer, you will need to market your skills and bring in your own clients. This provides a certain amount of flexibility and freedom, but marketing yourself is a time-consuming aspect of a freelancer's work. Also consider that your income as a freelancer is likely to be less stable than if you are employed by a company. Both options have their advantages and disadvantages, and some Web designers start out in one arena and move to the other as circumstances dictate. There is also a third option, which is working on one company's proprietary site as their in-house Web designer. This destination offers stability, but little variety, so consider your priorities for job satisfaction carefully.

Scout the terrain. Not surprisingly, most Web design positions are advertised online. A quick Google search for Web design jobs will turn up, literally, hundreds of sites soliciting résumés and advertising jobs around the globe. Due to the nature of the work, it may be possible for you to work remotely from the job location, an advantage if your locale is not a hotbed of technology employers. But some types of jobs will require that you liaise with the rest of your Web management team in person. In this case, your physical location is relevant and your willingness to move for a job may be determinative. If you want to freelance, the same rules apply: A company in Timbuktu may hire you to design their site and all communication may take place online. On the other hand, the best place to scout for Web design clients is close to home. Find out if local businesses have sites. If the already have one, do not let that deter you. If the site is outdated, you can offer to redo it or augment it with new features.

Essential Gear

Pack your portfolio. Although potential employers and clients will be interested in the academic and past experience credentials on your résumé, it is the portfolio of Web sites that you have designed that is your passport to a job. It does not matter what degrees you possess or where you have worked if your sites look amateurish, are difficult to navigate or do not function properly. No one is going to hire you until they see what you can do, so make sure that your portfolio shows off your design talents and technical skills.

Find the path that is right for you. Your background, interests, talents and financial situation are among the many factors that will help you set off on the right path to your new career in Web design. If you are more artistically inclined, your footsteps may lead you towards a more design-oriented focus, working on site layout, graphics, and ease of navigation. If you are more intrigued by the technical side of Web sites, you may choose to work behind the scenes, so to speak, on the programming aspects of a site. Both skill sets are equally necessary, and in demand, for the creation of a functional and appealing Web site.

Go back to school. If you have determined that you need more formal education to reach your new career destination, you could go back to school for a B.S. in Computer Science or Graphic Design. Some colleges and universities may have part-time or evening degree programs for non-traditional students that will enable you to attend classes around your current job. Keep in mind that your ability to get a Web design job depends more on your online portfolio than your formal credentials. The candidate with the site that blows away the competition is the one who will get the job, not the candidate with the list of degrees and online course credits.

Landmarks

If you are in your twenties . . . Then you might be well placed to start your journey to a Web design career with undergraduate or graduate courses in computer science or graphic design. At this stage of your life, you may have the flexibility to move for a suitable internship or job. Employers tend to assume that younger people are more computer savvy. Use this to your advantage, and develop your skills by designing as many sites as you can for practice.

If you are in your thirties or forties . . . You should assess how transferable your current job skills and experience are to the field of Web design. If you work in the visual arts, you can complement your design skills by taking some courses to learn the technical aspects of Web design. If your work is related to writing or editing, you could start by looking for a job in Web content management and work your way into site design. If you have an engineering or computer science background, the technical skills of Web design will probably be relatively easy for you to acquire.

If you are in your fifties . . . You could be in a position to go back to school either full or part-time to acquire a completely new skill set, regardless of your previous experience. Take advantage of this opportunity to acquire technical and business skills, if you can, but bear in mind that your portfolio counts more than your academic credentials. The best way to convince potential clients that you are the right designer to make their site is to have examples of attractive and skillfully done Web sites to show them.

If you are over sixty . . . You are going to be fighting the perception that younger people have a monopoly on computer skills. Show potential employers that this stereotype is unfounded by blowing them away with your cutting-edge portfolio. You could also tap into the growing market of older clients, such as boomers starting new businesses in retirement, who may be put off by working with snotty twenty-something Web designers.

Further Resources

Jennifer Kyrnin's Web Design/HTML Blog offers accessible and interesting advice on Web design, including information on keeping up with the latest trends, how to get a job, and where to find tutorials to learn new skills. http://webdesign.about.com/b

The World Wide Web Consortium are the Web gods who actually create CSS, HTML, XML and the other technologies used in Web design. Go, worship them. If this site does not answer your questions, the answer does not exist yet. http://www.w3.org

killersites.com provides information, including tutorials, on how to design and host Web sites. Site includes a discussion forum where you can get questions answered by other Web designers. http://www.killersites.com

The HTML Writers Guild offers online Web design training courses covering virtually every type of software and coding language commonly used in Web design. http://www.hwg.org

EBay Seller

Career Compasses

Get your bearings on what it takes to be a successful eBay seller.

Relevant Knowledge of the online auction market (20%)

Organizational Skills are crucial for keeping track of your auctions, inventory and sales (30%)

Mathematical Skills are necessary for calculating prices, fees, taxes, shipping, and all of the other financial calculations associated with online sales (30%)

Ability to Manage Stress is useful for dealing with the public. The customer is not always right, but they certainly always think that they are (20%)

Destination: EBay Seller

At first glance, this chapter may seem an odd choice for inclusion in a volume on changing careers. After all, everyone has sold something on eBay by now. It seems less of a career choice than a glorified garage sale, a way to get rid of those never-worn, final-sale-not-returnable red pumps that you bought in a size 6 even though you wear a 7. The sight of them was an annoying reminder of your poor judgment so you sold them to the highest bidder on eBay. The bidder, you notice, had used the "e-mail seller" feature to ask you if they run large because she wears a 6.

If that type of scenario is what comes to mind when you think of selling on eBay, you may wonder how it fits as a career option. Well, at the other end of the spectrum from the casual eBayer is the eBay Power Seller, merchants who have, at the Bronze level, a minimum of $1,000 in sales per month, up to the Diamond level, with monthly sales of $500,000 or more. Power Sellers make up only about 4 percent of all eBay sellers, but that is still quite a few merchants who are making a good chunk of their living from eBay sales. Would you like to join them? Launching a career in eBay sales is similar to building a Web site for your business and selling online, with some important distinctions. If you sell items on your own Web site, you probably have fixed prices for them. EBay gives you the option of selling items at a fixed price or offering them at auction. If you are concerned about your items selling for too little, you can set a reserve price or a starting bid.

Essential Gear

Snap a photo, clinch a deal. It may seem like a pain to stage and photograph your items, but take a look at some listings with photographs and some without, and see which ones sell, and for what price. It is already risky for a potential buyer to bid on an item that they have not seen in person, and send money to a stranger in the hope that they will send it to them. Think how much riskier that transaction becomes if you have to take the stranger's word for the color, condition, and other details of the merchandise. In fact, many bidders exclude from consideration listings without photos. EBay lets you include one picture in your listing for free; you can add up to eleven additional pictures for a small fee. You can have eBay host your pictures or link from another site. If you do not have a digital camera, invest in one (hey, you could buy one on eBay) because a cell phone will usually not take high quality photos.

EBay offers a range of seller tools for managing your listings and selling at auction or at a fixed price, giving you an opportunity to take your existing business online without setting up an e-commerce Web site of your own. It is a convenient way to test the waters of online sales, but it does not come free. EBay charges a flat insertion fee to place your listing, which is based upon the starting or reserve price, and a final value fee, which is a percentage of the closing price. Currently, these fees are as high as 15 percent, and some sellers have left eBay out of a conviction that they cannot make a profit. There are additional fees for upgrading listings, hosting pictures, and special fee structures for vehicle and real estate listings and eBay Stores. There are also taxes and shipping charges to be considered. But do not let the costs alone discourage you. Depending upon the market for your type of merchandise, you may be able to supplement your current income or even, if you are a savvy e-business marketer, make a living from your eBay income. The barriers to entry are low so there really is no reason not to give eBay selling a try. Read on for everything you need to know to get the bidding started.

You Are Here

You can begin your journey to eBay selling from many different locales.

Do you have something to sell? To state the obvious, eBay is a giant e-commerce Web site. People go there for one of two reasons: to sell stuff or to buy stuff. It is the people who are selling stuff that are making money, at least in theory. So, what are you going to sell? If you currently have a store, you can try listing some of your merchandise on eBay. If your merchandise is not easily shippable, you will be limited to local buyers, but it might still increase your customer base beyond those who know about your physical store. If you pursue an art or craft, you can list some of your creations. But if you do not have merchandise and you are thinking of buying inventory just to launch a career selling on eBay, do yourself a big favor and educate yourself about eBay's recent problems and substantial fall-off in sales before you invest a penny.

Do you have basic computer skills? Selling on eBay does not require advanced programming skills. It is certainly easier for the computer neophyte than launching his or her own e-commerce site. But it does take a certain amount of basic computer knowledge to navigate the seller tools, upload digital photographs, and utilize PayPal for processing payments. To jazz up your listings so that they catch the eye of potential buyers, you will need some basic HTML skills. If you are not yet comfortable navigating online and uploading from/downloading to your computer, brush up your computer skills by asking a computer-savvy friend or family member, getting some books, using online tutorials, or taking a basic computer literacy course.

Do you know how much work this is going to be? It sounds so simple to list an item and sell it, with little overhead, commuting, or other hassles, but it actually takes quite a bit of time to manage eBay auctions. Staging and photographing your merchandise, uploading and Photoshopping your pictures, writing an effective listing, monitoring the listing, answering queries from bidders, packing and posting the item to the winner, dealing with suppliers, distributors, drop-shippers, and other middlemen, and keeping good records of all transactions, is time consuming. If you paid yourself a minimum hourly wage for these tasks, you might find your profits disappearing.

Navigating the Terrain

Organizing Your Expedition

Before you set out, know where you are going.

Decide on a destination. It should be obvious that selling on eBay can fit into your life in various ways. It could be an occasional supplement to your current income, a regular part of your sales, or your exclusive business domain. The vast majority of the 1.3 million sellers on eBay, about 650,000 of whom are in the United States, do not make a living exclusively from their eBay sales. Even Bronze and Silver level Power Sellers certainly must supplement their income somehow. Some have unrelated jobs, and many have their own brick-and-mortar stores or e-commerce Web sites. There was a heyday several years ago when eBay was so popular with consumers that some popular sellers of items like DVDs were able to turn massive profits with a distributor and a packing and shipping operation. But those days have ended, at least for the foreseeable future. A more realistic plan is to make a portion of your living from your eBay sales, as a supplement to your current income, and see where the economy and your business go in the future.

Essential Gear

Consider Your Bidder. There are two ways you can ensure that a minimum price is met for your item: setting a starting bid and naming a reserve price. A starting bid is visible to potential buyers, and may put them off even clicking on your listing, whereas a reserve price is never visible to the bidder. All the bidders see is a "reserve not met" notice by the latest bid until the reserve is met, then the notice disappears and there is no indication that the listing ever had a reserve price. When you set a reserve price, you can place a low starting bid to generate interest in your listing. When buyers click on it and read the description and see the pictures, they may be moved to bid—something that would not happen if a high starting bid discourages them from even clicking.

Scout the terrain. In this case, the terrain is the Internet, and you are scouting for other businesses that sell the same type of merchandise that you do. Search for your product on eBay. Are there a lot of sellers? A few sellers with many items? Is your type of merchandise available? If it is not to be found, first do a quick check of eBay policies to be sure that it is not a prohibited item. The question that will be harder to answer is whether the absence is indicative of a market niche you could fill or a lack of interest from consumers that have driven businesses like yours away. The only way to find out is to list some items and see if anyone bids.

Find the path that is right for you. The only way to find out if eBay selling is suitable for you and your merchandise is to set up an eBay Seller Account and list some items. The process is very simple, with clear instructions given on site. You can play around with titles and descriptions, shipping charges, photographs of your merchandise, length of auctions, reserve prices and starting bids, read tips on getting your listings noticed, and tweak your selling tactics over time, based on trial and error. It may take awhile to find out which selling techniques are best for your merchandise, so try to be patient and pay attention to the traffic on your listings.

Go back to school. The only reason you would have to go back to school to enhance your career in eBay sales would be for further training in your craft if you are selling merchandise that you make yourself. If you are, for example, an artist such as a painter, sculptor, or photographer who is selling your work on eBay, you might think that attending art school would enhance your artistic skills and increase your sales. Or perhaps you sell refurbished electronic equipment and you wish to go to trade school or obtain an apprenticeship to become a licensed electrician. Other than a scenario like that, there are no educational or degree requirements to sell on eBay. Anyone who can use a computer can do it.

Landmarks

If you are in your twenties . . . Age is not a relevant factor in entering this career, except in the sense that younger merchants who have grown up with the Internet are likely to be more comfortable buying and selling online. Put your computer skills to good use by making your listing stand out with high quality digital photographs and utilizing eBay's listing management tools.

If you are in your thirties or forties . . . You can start small by listing a few items as a sideline to your current business. You do not have to

Notes from the Field

Eric Armour
EBay seller
San Diego, California

What were you doing before you decided to change careers?

At the time that I started selling on eBay, I was in restaurant management. I have an associate's degree in architecture and I practiced for seven years in Washington, D.C. upon graduation, then I was a real estate agent in the metro Norfolk, Virginia area. In 1996, I moved to San Diego, California, to be an apprentice to an armorer in Hollywood. That didn't work out. But I kept making armor. In fact, I had made armor as a hobby since college. Even though I was treating restaurant management as a career, I made it clear that as soon as the armoring broke out, I was out of there. I wanted to be a full-time armorer, but the work wasn't there locally and I wasn't computer literate. I tried eBay in June of 2000 as an experiment. Everything I put there sold. Back then, when you put in a search for Society for Creative Anachronism (SCA) armor, most of it was old, warn out garbage that wasn't even legal for SCA combat, and then there was my stuff. At first, there was a service that would automatically list stuff. They're long since out of business and now eBay provides that service free. I started by putting up my 10 biggest sellers at Renaissance fairs and the like automatically every two weeks and everything was selling.

Why did you change your career?

It seemed like a natural way to increase my business.

How did you make the transition?

Out of the gates on eBay, I matched my 40-hour-week restaurant take-home pay with 20 hours in the shop. That continued, while I was simul-

leave your current job to become an eBay seller. If business becomes so good and steady that you could dive in to selling exclusively on eBay, you might want to consider the long term before jumping ship. Always have a back-up plan if eBay sales drop off.

If you are in your fifties . . . You might be thinking of setting up an e-commerce site for your current business but want to dip your toe into taneously under increasing pressure to take more and more promotions at the restaurant or get out. EBay sales were increasing 10 percent a year and there just was not room for both. It was difficult for me to leave a stable job to pursue my armoring.

What are the keys to success in your new career?

First, I feel obliged to tell you that I was one of the first armorers to sell on eBay in 2000 but I have since stopped selling there. Since April of 2008, eBay has been involved in some serious problems, and they treat their sellers so badly that it is not a viable business model to sell there anymore. Now, as to success, eventually, I learned to use the marketing skills I had picked up in real estate. I never let a deal die until I get a firm "no." I publicize my activity on many message boards, living history forums, etc. I'd post these on forums and generate 800 hits on my armor per day. Armor sales began to grow at 20-30 percent after I left the restaurant. It was a well-oiled machine.

[Also] I do everything according to a schedule. A lot of armorers have attention span problems. By changing [armoring] activities every 20 minutes, it kept my focus, kept my attention span, and kept my body from wearing out.

But then [in 2008, eBay made policy changes that negatively impacted my business. This was followed by the economic downturn] I did have to take a part-time job, and I will keep it regardless of what the armory does until I see some definite signs that this recession is over. I am still in transition because eBay is still a mess. It has a rapidly decreasing reputation. I am on a site called Bonanzle, which I think will ultimately be the winner to supplant eBay in the United States. I am also on eBid, which is a privately owned company out of London. I think they will be the company that ultimately supplants eBay in Europe.

online sales without having to put up your own Web site. EBay, and its growing competition from other online auction sites, provides just such an opportunity.

If you are over sixty . . . You could be in the same position described for the fifty-somethings, above, or perhaps you are retiring and would like to turn a hobby into a business by selling crafts or other items that you make online. EBay selling is a great way to expand your customer base beyond your local area, and to generate income from a home-based business.

Further Resources

Platinum Power Seller.com sells software and tutorials to help start your own online selling business on eBay.   http://www.bigwebmaster. com

Tips On Marketing.com contains a step-by-step tutorial on how to become a registered eBay seller.   http://www.tipsonmarketing.com/Become _an_eBay_Seller

E-Commerce Merchants Trade Organization is a trade association for online retailers, not just eBay sellers.   http://www.ecmta.org

Web Entrepreneur

Web Entrepreneur

Career Compasses

Get your bearings on what it takes to be a successful Web entrepreneur.

Relevant Knowledge of your industry and its online market (30%)

Organizational Skills are essential for any small business owner who runs the whole show alone (25%)

Mathematical Skills are also a useful asset for anyone in the business world (20%)

Ability to Manage Stress is key to launching any successful new business, whether or not it is online (25%)

Destination: Web Entrepreneur

What do Drew Curtis (Fark.com), Scott Heiferman (Meetup.com), Stephen Chao (WonderHowTo.com), Jeremy "ShoeMoney" Schoemaker (ShoeMoney Media Group), and, perhaps someday, you have in common? They are all Web entrepreneurs who have founded hugely popular Web sites or Web services that have made them rich and famous. Okay, comfortably well-off and moderately famous, but they are all still busy dreaming up new ideas and expanding their virtual empires. It is easy to see the appeal of becoming a Web entrepreneur. Before the Web, an entrepreneur needed physical space for a business, as well as a lot of capital for inventory and advertising. And if you lived in New York, attracting customers in California, Singapore, or Paris was a challenge even after your business was well-established. The advent of the Internet changed the playing field for entrepreneurs. Now all you need is a computer, an idea, a hosting service, and some technical skills to put them all together. The barriers to entry are lower, and the start-up capital needed much less; however, just like most off-line entrepreneurial ventures fail, most online ones do not become the next Google or Facebook. What makes an online business venture a success? For some Web entrepreneurs, it seems that not setting out to make money was a key component of their success.

Essential Gear

Learn the local lingo. Every profession has industry-specific terminology that is opaque to outsiders, but no era in history has given us as many new terms as the technological revolution. Consider the following sentence: "Check your mobile, I just e-mailed you a hyperlink to that wiki I've been blogging about." It is perfectly intelligible today, yet most of its nouns and verbs did not exist or had different meanings as recently as 15 years ago. To be a successful Web entrepreneur, you must be fluent in the Web 2.0 dialect or risk sounding like a Luddite technophobe, which is not a great way to inspire confidence in your employees or investors. Remember: the first step to knowing what you are doing is sounding as if you do.

Many were the first to start a certain type of online service, and others were not first, but offered a way to do something better. A tiny minority saw a profitable market niche and exploited it. Before we go over some of the skills, talents, and experience that you will need to start your own Web-based business, let us take a brief glimpse at a few Web success stories for inspiration and edification.

The information age is notorious for overwhelming us with useless and repetitive news. Alas, Drew Curtis's Fark.com is not helping to relieve that cacophony but it is at least making it funnier. Fark.com began when Drew was studying abroad and began e-mailing weird news stories to his friends back home. Eventually he decided to index them on a Web site, with forums provided for users to argue about them. Drew no longer posts all of the headlines himself. Instead, Fark has a submission tool for users to attempt their clever take on headlines for the news links of the day, and a team of admins to "greenlight" the funniest headlines for the Fark.com homepage. The overarching theme of the site, and of Curtis's bestselling book, *It's Not News, It's FARK*, is that the mass media is spoon-feeding us non-news as news and we are eating it up. In contrast to many Web entrepreneurs who cluster in tech meccas such as Silicon Valley and New York, Curtis resides in Kentucky. As a Web entrepreneur, Curtis had the advantage of having owned and run an ISP, so he knew a bit about servers and hosting. Another key to the site's success, aside from its irresistible appeal to cubicle drones for wasting time at work, is that it has diversified its revenue streams. There are classified ads on the site, as well as advertisements, and users can pay a monthly fee to view and comment on stories in the submission queue. As long as people want to waste time arguing on the Internet, there will be a place for Fark.com.

Essential Gear

Get touched by an angel. No, not the kind with halos and wings, the kind with checkbooks and deep pockets. If you have some coding skills, you can do much of the work to get your Web site up and running on your own, but you will need to pay a monthly charge for hosting services and to advertise and market your new site to generate traffic, among many, many other expenses as your site grows. The amount of start-up capital that you will need will vary depending upon your technical skills, connections, and the site's purpose and functionality, but $250,000 is a figure that comes up a lot in interviews with Web entrepreneurs when they are asked how much angel investor seed money they needed to begin.

Some Web entrepreneurs have tried to find ways that the Web can be used to enhance our off-line lives rather than as an end in itself. Scott Heiferman, CEO and founder of Meetup.com, thought it would be a good idea to harness the communications ability to the Internet to facilitate the matching of people to others in their local community with similar interests by providing an interface for organizing meetings. In a world where electronic communication is replacing face-to-face contact, Meetup.com facilitates community spirit. Unlike other Web 2.0 sites that are supported exclusively through advertising revenue, Meetup.com charges group organizers a small monthly fee. Its sound business plan and worldwide success have enabled Heiferman to keep enhancing the site so that it has evolved significantly since its founding in 2002. A key lesson to take from Meetup.com's story is that you cannot launch a Web enterprise and leave it static even if its initial incarnation is a huge success. In order to hold onto your users, you must listen to them and respond to their needs. And the most important message from Meetup.com is that helping people is the best measure of success.

Stephen Chao observed that resourceful do-it-yourselfers have been turning to online searches for tutorials on how to do everything from conventional home repair and cooking to tying sailors' knots or tuning a mandolin. He thought it would be convenient to compile the vast number of instructional videos on the Internet into one Web site, so he did, and he called it WonderHowTo.com, as in, "Did you ever wonder how to...?" The site functions as a search engine that trolls over 1,700 informational Web sites with video tutorials, and as a compendium of video tutorials categorized by general subject such as "Arts & Crafts," "Family," and "Magic & Parlor Tricks." Note that he is not providing any original content, not even a "how to be a Web entrepreneur" video based upon his own experiences. All of the site's content is hosted elsewhere. His goal is to index all of the free how-to videos on the Web. The site's traffic shot up from 100,000 unique views per day to upwards of 800,000 within several months of its launch, helping to ensure a steady stream of advertising revenue, the income source for most free Web sites. If you think about it, you could Google "how to open a champagne bottle with a sword" and get the same video direct from the content provider. WonderHowTo.com is merely indexing a subset of Web content so that users will search it, and see its ads, rather than using a general search engine. Also, the index enables you to browse how-to videos and find out how to do things, such as make a wallet out of tape, for which it might never occur to you to search. Whether this is a good thing or not is for you to decide; the point is that someone is making money at it.

You are probably used to seeing advertisements along the borders, and sometimes inserted between sections of content, on most Web sites. But this was not always the case. When the Web was young, the initial thinking was that revenue for non-e-commerce sites would come from charging users to view content. This formula works for some types of content, pornography by far the most successful of them, but it failed to catch on in other sectors. Consumers simply were not willing to pay for most content, and Web entrepreneurs had to come up with some other way to generate income. Jeremy "ShoeMoney" Schoemaker, founder of

ShoeMoney Media Group, was not the first person to think of employing targeted advertisements on Web sites, but he has applied that idea, and many other ideas for generating income from affiliate and search engine marketing, into considerable success as a Web entrepreneur. One of his most prominent ventures was AuctionAds, a service that places eBay auction ads on relevant Web sites.

You Are Here

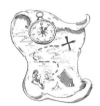

You can begin your journey to Web entrepreneurship from many different locales.

Do you have offline experience in your proposed online business? No, it is not required, but many online businesses are extensions of real world occupations, and knowing your industry is a useful starting point. Arianna Huffington, founder of The Huffington Post, a popular newsblog Web site, was a well-known author and syndicated columnist before she started her online business. Her journalistic experience was a tremendous asset in choosing aggregated news content and other topics for her Web site, and in attracting prominent journalists, authors, public officials and other celebrities to write for it.

Do you have the technical skills to build your site? If your initial response to this query is, "I can hire people," think again. It is true that you will need staff to help you develop and run your Web-based business, and no-one individual is proficient in every type of Web technology; however, a strong technical background is necessary for you to know what functionality is possible, and at what cost.

Are you an entrepreneur? This is the most critical question to ask yourself. Business and technical skills can be acquired but nothing will change your innate temperament and talents. Not everyone is cut out to run his or her own business. Researchers have studied entrepreneurs and they tend to share certain traits. Entrepreneurs, not surprisingly, tend to be visionary people, and they need good communication skills to communicate their vision. They also tend to be obsessive, hyper-focused, and can eat, sleep, and breathe their idea without respite for an indefinite period of

Navigating the Terrain

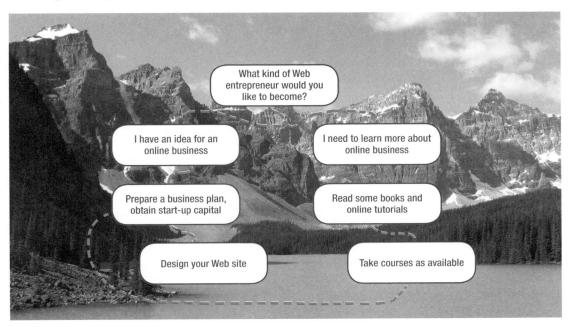

time. Most notably, entrepreneurs tend to have a higher level of self-confidence than other members of society. This seems logical as confidence is necessary to convince both yourself and others that your idea is worth the time, effort and resources it will take to bring it to fruition.

Organizing Your Expedition

Before you set out, know where you are going.

Decide on a destination. Are you ready to start your own business? Answering that question is not straightforward because often we do not know what we do not know. You first need an idea for a Web-based business that does not yet exist or an idea for providing an existing service better. But the raw idea is just the beginning. You need to figure out the technical aspects of making your idea a reality, and you need to assess the costs so you can develop a business plan that will seem like a good

Notes from the Field
Kelly Lockhart
Web entrepreneur
Chattanooga, Tennessee

What were you doing before you decided to change careers?
I was a reporter for a local news network.

Why did you change your career?
Budget and staffing cutbacks decimated the newsroom, and the hand-writing on the wall showed that it was only going to get worse. Plus, I was getting very turned off by the ever-growing corporate control over the news—what was chosen to air and how it was presented, and how the sales department seemed increasingly to be dictating what was focused upon.

investment to potential funders. Although this tool is not geared exclusively toward Web-based businesses, this questionnaire will help you assess your readiness for starting your own business: http://www.sba.gov/assessmenttool/index.html.

Scout the terrain. It should go without saying that your first task is to thoroughly search the Web to ensure that your idea has not already been implemented. Once you are convinced that your idea is novel, do some research into its potential market. Who are you expecting to utilize your products or services? Is this market out there? How do you know there is latent demand for it? At several stages in your business development process, you may want to arrange focus groups to get feedback on your site's appeal to potential users. Pay careful attention to what they say, but do not feel that you have to utilize every suggestion.

Find the path that is right for you. Your journey to the launch of your own Web-based business will vary, but certain steps will be common to

How did you make the transition?

I resigned, registered a domain name, hired a competent Web developer to build an independent news Web site and began working from home.

What are the keys to success in your new career?

In my case, the Web site has been successful because it has created an active community. The message forum part of the site is incredibly active. We host monthly parties around town and are involved in a wide variety of charity and social events. I work closely with both the established and independent media in town, many of whom feed stories to us that they cannot get on the air or in print themselves. I also keep costs low so that I only need a limited number of advertisers to turn a reasonable profit. And I have constantly tweaked and adjusted the Web site to meet the interests of the visitors—adding comics that weren't carried locally, for example, or giving the former restaurant reviewer for the city paper an online home to continue her popular reviews.

most. First you will need to find a hosting service and ensure that it is compatible with your site's proposed functionality and traffic. Then you need to design your Web site. You may need to hire people to help you with this part, so this is where start-up capital becomes crucial. Once the site is ready to launch, you will need to develop a strategy for marketing it. Many Web entrepreneurs find ways to promote their site virally so that they do not need to spend money on advertising. What works for you will depend upon your resources, the strength of your idea, and a little bit of luck.

Go back to school. Since you are embarking on your own business adventure, you will be the boss, which means you do not have to worry about potential employers scrutinizing your résumé for any particular educational requirements. In fact, quite a few Web entrepreneurs have dropped out of school and never completed their degrees when their sites demanded their full-time attention. Although he was not a Web entrepreneur exactly, you can count Bill Gates amongst that number.

That said, if you lack certain business or technical skills that are critical or even just advisable for launching your own business, you could look into taking a few courses, although not necessarily in a degree-seeking program. There are plenty of stand-alone business, finance, and technical courses offered in the evenings or online for non-degree-seeking students. An MBA is more likely to be geared toward running a large company, but plenty of business courses are pitched at small business owners and teach skills like preparing a business plan, marketing, accounting, and employee management. Nowadays, there are courses specifically targeted to e-commerce. Even if you plan on hiring Web designers and coders, you need to have much more than a basic familiarity with HTML to run a Web-based business. You need to be acquainted with networks, databases, hosting, security, programming, the most commonly used scripting languages, and the basic architecture of the Web. An incredibly comprehensive and organized list of Web technology tutorial information can be found here: http://www.khake.com/page65.html. This site also includes extensive links to useful business skills tutorials and other resources for careers in e-commerce.

Landmarks

If you are in your twenties . . . There are probably some essential prerequisites to starting your own online business that you possess. Odds are that you have an idea, confidence, and some technical skills, but that you lack a detailed business plan and start-up capital. You are going to need to write the former to get the latter, so research how to make a sound business plan and get started on it.

If you are in your thirties or forties . . . You are probably in a slightly better position than a twenty-something in the sense that you will have built up more business and technical skills, as well as useful connections. One possible obstacle for your age group is that you may have family obligations and expenses that might make taking the leap to starting your own business more fraught with risk. It is important to remember that, for online businesses, success is measured more in traffic than in income, and a successful Web site may take years to turn a profit, if it ever does.

If you are in your fifties . . . And your kids are grown and your mortgage is paid, you may be better-placed than younger Web entrepreneurs to take a leap of faith and quit your day job to launch your Web venture. It will help if you have savings on which to live—you will need it.

If you are over sixty . . . Since you are going into business for yourself, you do not have to worry about age discrimination or the perception from potential employers that younger hires are more tech savvy and tuned into online culture; however, you may have to deal with this attitude from potential investors. On the other hand, your business experience will give you an advantage and help you avoid unrealistic expectations. Life will have taught you that there are no legitimate get-rich-quick schemes, and that launching any business takes time and hard work.

Further Resources

Web-Entrepreneur.com is a paid subscription site that is geared toward e-commerce business owners. Its information is more relevant to established business owners, but it does contain some fundamentals for newbies. http://web-entrepreneur.com/index.php
Entrepreneur.com is all about starting your own online business. http://www.entrepreneur.com
Tech Republic compiles articles and other resources for Web entrepreneurs. http://search.techrepublic.com.com/search/entrepreneur.html
Inside CRM provides customer relationship management resources and information for online sales and marketing. http://www.insidecrm.com

Web Publicist/ Blogger

Web Publicist/Blogger

Career Compasses

Get your bearings on what it takes to be a successful Web publicist/blogger.

Relevant Knowledge of the topic or subject about which you are blogging or that you are publicizing (30%)

Caring about your blog and its subject matter will give it credibility and help to retain your interest (10%)

Communication Skills in their written form are essential (50%)

Ability to Manage Stress never hurts, particularly when you have to deal with negative feedback from readers (10%)

Destination: Web Publicist/Blogger

Let us establish something right from the beginning: you are not going to make your living as a blogger. The idea of being able to work anywhere you have your laptop and WiFi, composing missives full of wit and wisdom for which the teeming masses will pay you handsomely is pure fantasy. And there is no such thing as a Web publicist. Traditional publicists must take advantage of the Web to promote their clients, and they must monitor what is out on the Web about their clients for damage control, but no publicist works exclusively online.

Though there are a few bloggers who are paid for their posts, most of them were well-known in their field prior to blogging. In fact, blogging is often a public relations tool that they use to promote themselves; it is not income generating on its own. Most celebrities have blogs, which are places where they can announce information about upcoming shows, appearances, releases, etc., and where they can counteract rumors in the press and post links to places where fans can purchase their CDs, videos, books, or other merchandise. These blogs are marketing tools more than personal journals, and the level of personalized content that the celebrity provides varies considerably. Now that you have been disabused of the notion that you can make money from a blog, let us consider what you can do with a blog.

Blogs come in different types, and have varied uses. The first type of blog that probably leaps to mind when you consider the concept is an online diary. For people born and raised before the information age, it is sometimes difficult to understand why someone would want to post their personal journal for the public to see. A traditional diary is often kept under lock and key. Indeed, most blogging software allows you to adjust privacy settings to control who can read your blog, but keeping it completely private sort of defeats the purpose of putting it on the Web in the first place. The popularity of online diary Web sites like LiveJournal (http://www.livejournal.com) demonstrates that there is a

Essential Gear

Be the ruler of your new domain. Most blog hosting sites are free but the URL for your blog incorporates the host's name, e.g. www.my supercooltravelblog.blogspot.com or www. livejournal.com/mybloggityblog. A truly professional looking blog needs its own URL. It looks better, sounds better, and it is easier to remember. First you need to come up with a catchy, clever and memorable name for your blog, and then you need to find out if that domain is available. You can try typing it into your browser but even if the site is inactive, it may be registered to someone else. Try using http://www.whois. com to find out if it is available. There are a variety of domain registration services. They all do the same thing, but at varying prices, so you may want to shop around before you pick one. Another thing to consider is registering various extensions to protect your site from being imitated. That is, even if you are intending to use only myblogname.com, also register myblog name.net, myblogname.org, etc.

latent exhibitionist streak in all of us. Well, at least in those of us under 25, who represent the majority of the sixteen million strong LiveJournal community. It is no coincidence that LiveJournal was founded in 1999 by a high school student for the purpose of keeping his friends abreast of his activities. Unlike the old-fashioned paper sort, online diaries can be illustrated with pictures and livened up with many kinds of audio/visual materials and links to other Web sites. Another feature unique to online diaries is that they provide space for readers to comment on the entries. There is also a community aspect to online journals in that people can join friend lists or subscribe to specific blogs, thus keeping their friends up-to-date with their latest moods and ruminations on life, the universe, and everything. Joining an online virtual journal community such as LiveJournal is usually free, but you may have to tolerate advertisements on your diary.

Although personal blogs are the most common type of blog, they are far from the only type out there in the blogosphere. Political blogs are also quite popular, and can be founded by laypeople as well as academics and journalists. In fact, political blogs are so common that there is now a blurring of the blogosphere and the mainstream media. People are increasingly turning to blogs for their news because they believe bloggers provide first-person accounts of world events, photographs, and information that is not filtered and sanitized as it is in the mainstream media. Some of the more well-known political blogs include The Daily Dish, Wonkette, and Daily Kos. A few political blogs are so widely read that they have brought fame to their founders, who now appear regularly on radio and televisions as political pundits. Some people blog about their jobs, such as international correspondents and military personnel, but they are subject to the oversight of their employers who can fire them or demand that they not publish certain information. There is not shortage of travel blogs, cooking blogs, legal blogs, knitting blogs, music blogs, and blogs on virtually every subject under the sun. Blogging is beginning to serve as a way to keep alive dying languages, particularly the Gaelic languages. There are fan blogs devoted to celebrities and themed blogs devoted to sports, specific sports teams, and other subjects. There is no limit to the topics that you could blog about, with the exception of content that is considered libelous, obscene, or otherwise illegal.

Not all blogs are written. Blogs can convey their information through photographs, called photoblogs; videos, known as vlogs; audio, called podcasts; drawings, dubbed sketchblogs, music, via MP3 blogs, and micro-blogging, which uses very brief posts, akin to text messages. Podcasts quickly grew in popularity after the advent of the iPhone, and photo and video blogs have become quite common. Most written blogs can contain other embedded content when the blogger chooses to add it, such as photographs and video clips. It is interesting to contemplate what new form blogs will take as technology advances.

You Are Here

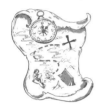

You can begin your journey to Web publicizing/blogging from many different locales.

Are you a writer? If you are not already a writer, starting a blog will certainly give you practice and develop your writing skills. But remember that no one is editing your blog. Unless you get feedback from readers, you will not improve your clarity, style, and grammar without the sort of editorial comments you get as a professional or serious amateur writer. If you were a journalist, staff would edit and proofread your work before it appeared in print. Spelling and grammatical errors, not to mention poor writing, will turn people off from reading your blog. Likewise, if you blog in some other form, such as video, audio, or photo, make sure that your filmmaking, photography, or oratorical skills show you off to advantage.

Are you famous? Or at least really good at something? Think about how you hear of blogs. They are either written by people you know or people you have heard of. If you start a blog today, how are you going to build an audience? Savvy marketing and an advertising budget will help, and it is particularly important not to underestimate the efficacy of viral marketing in the information age, but you still need a hook. Time is a commodity just like money. What is going to cause people to spend it on your blog? If your name is known outside of the blogosphere, it can be a great kick-start. If not, do not despair, just be conscious that marketing your blog is going to require patience, diligence, and a bit of good luck.

Do you have basic HTML skills? Most blogging software is simple to use, but your blog is not going to stand out from the other 200,000 million or so blogs in the blogosphere unless you are able to customize it.

Navigating the Terrain

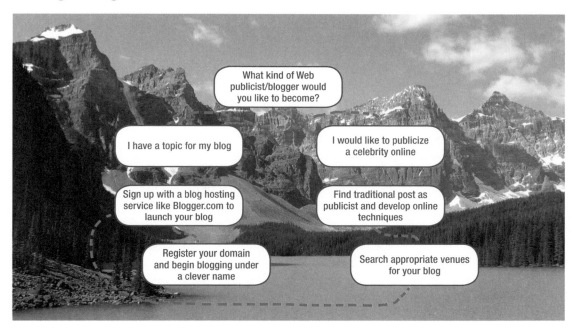

Some bloggers make their own Web sites for their blogs independently but even a blog on a site like Blogger can be customized so extensively that it looks unique. If you register your own domain name, you can even host your blog elsewhere so it points to your domain name instead of to the Blogger (or other blog hosting service) URL. A professional looking blog needs its own domain.

Organizing Your Expedition

Before you set out, know where you are going.

Decide on a destination. As you begin your journey into the blogosphere, you will have a few decisions to make. The first is to decide upon the medium in which you wish to blog. That choice will dictate some of your available software and hosting options. Most blogs are written, you have a variety of free and low-cost hosting options for this medium,

Stories from the Field

Andrew Sullivan
Blogger, http://www.andrewsullivan.com
Washington, D.C.

Andrew Sullivan has the rare distinction of being paid to write his blog. Before you begin to leap about with joy and shout, "I knew it could be done!", consider Sullivan's career trajectory. He was born and raised in England and received a first class honors degree from Oxford University and then earned both an MPA and Ph.D. from Harvard. He began writing for The New Republic, *a conservative magazine, in 1986, and was promoted to editor, serving from 1991 to 1996, when he left under somewhat of a cloud after losing a power struggle. During his tenure, he made some controversial editorial choices that contributed to his notoriety. He then wrote for* The New York Times Magazine *and other prominent publications. Sullivan has also written five books. He has been a guest on many news and political commentary television shows, and remains an oddity as a British citizen who devotes his professional life to the study of American politics. He achieved considerable fame in part from his seemingly contradictory political views. He labels himself as a conservative and a Roman Catholic, and he takes traditionally conservative or libertarian stances on many prominent policy issues, including a hawkish military posture, yet he is a very outspoken advocate of gay rights and he married his gay partner in Massachusetts. He initially supported former president George W. Bush and the invasion of Iraq, but*

including Blogger, LiveJournal, WordPress, Xanga, TypePad, MySpace, Vox, and others. Standard blog software will allow you to post photographs but if you want to make a photoblog you may be better off with Fotolog, Flickr, or another photolog service that is designed specifically for that purpose. The most popular site for videoblogs is YouTube. There used to be quite a few MP3 blog sites, but MySpace seems to be taking over that market even though it was not designed for that purpose and limits artists to uploading only six MP3s at a time. Podcasts are usually available via a subscription service using a syndication protocol such as changed his mind as events progressed. Whereas early in his career he debated liberals, atheists, and even gay rights activists, he now seems to have much more in common with the left than the right and the label of conservative no longer seems appropriate. His views are closest to modern libertarianism, although he is always full of surprises that generate reader interest and discussion.

Sullivan began writing his blog, *The Daily Dish*, in 2000. In 2006, he wrote it officially for *Time Magazine*, switching to the *Atlantic Monthly* in 2007, when he accepted an editorial position, where it remains today. The success of Sullivan's blog is partly due to his pre-existing fame as a political journalist, and partly to timing. He was one of the first major political journalists to start blogging, and the 9/11 terrorist attack brought him considerable traffic. The traffic on his blog is enormous, with well over 50,000 unique page hits per day. He blogs about American politics, especially gay rights issues, and he gives out annual parody awards in a variety of categories for various forms of egregious political statements.

Note that Sullivan's income derives from books, articles, columns, speaking engagements and his editorial posts, not his blog *per se*. He has accepted sponsorships for his blog, sometimes controversially as when he was sponsored by a pharmaceutical company that makes drugs to combat AIDS. In his characteristic way, he rebutted the criticism by stating that the industry was saving his life, as he is HIV positive. The main lesson to take away from Sullivan's success is that you need to achieve your fame and earn your income in ways tangential to your blog, that it is an adjunct to a successful career, not a career ladder in itself.

RSS. The major up-and-coming micro-blogging service is Twitter, a social networking site that limits posts, called "Tweets" to 140 characters. Brevity may be the soul of wit, but a more likely explanation for this site's growing usage is the short-attention span of the twenty-first century information consumer.

Scout the terrain. Once you have picked your blogging medium and blog host, you will need to decide on a theme or topic for you blog. If it just going to be an online dairy, that step might not be necessary, but since this is nominally a chapter about blogging as a career, you need to find a specific topic for your blog that will appeal to people other than your closest friends and relatives. If you can blog about your current field of expertise, that is ideal. Are you a professional chef? Then consider starting a cooking blog. If you are a professional or highly skilled amateur photographer, you might orient your blog towards teaching people how to take good photographs, using your own work to illustrate your tips with examples. You can also chronicle your experiences in your job, but be very careful of this angle because, no matter how carefully you try to anonymize your blog, employees tend to find them and the employer is *always* fired, with little legal recourse. You may even be sued for libel by your former employer, or even by a former lover, if you reveal unflattering details.

Essential Gear

Reel in subscribers. Even readers who love your blog and bookmark it may forget to check for new postings, especially if they appear at irregular intervals, so make it easy for people to follow your blog by enabling them to subscribe to an RSS feed. Most blogging software offers you the option of adding a button to your site to enable visitors to your blog's RSS feed to sign up so they will be notified when the blog is updated. This is a great way to increase your readership because users of the feed will be reminded of your blog's existence, and they may forward interesting posts to their friends, who may then also sign up for the feed, and so on.

Find the path that is right for you. Blogging should be fun. If it is a chore to update your blog and you find yourself posting anything just to fulfill your duty or you go for long periods without updates, you might want to reconsider whether maintaining a blog is right for you. On the other hand, getting acquainted with the software and the medium, and developing the habit will also take time, so do not give up too soon.

Go back to school. You do not need any particular educational credentials to become a blogger. The whole point is that anyone can do it: Anyone can be a journalist, columnist, author, writer, poet, photographer, expert, teacher, and chronicler online because you do not need to show any qualifications to anyone to start a blog. Even if you are a novice doing your first DIY project in your first house, you can publish step-by-step instructions on your blog, as if you were a DIY expert. The catch, of course, is that readers might be more willing to take your advice seriously if you have some credentials and experience in your blog's subject. In fact, it helps a lot if you are already famous when you start your blog. Since there is no money in blogging, going to journalism school just so people will take your political blog seriously would be a bad idea. Also, blog hosting services make the process of starting and maintaining a blog so easy that you do not need any computer skills. If you want to host your blog independently and customize it, you might consider taking a basic HTML or Web design course. There are many such courses available, appropriately enough, online.

Landmarks

If you are in your twenties . . . Get thee a blog right now. Just do it. Check out a few blog hosting sites and create a free account with whichever one appeals to you. There is no reason why you cannot have more than one blog, so make this first one experimental. You can develop it or delete it as you find your blogging niche.

If you are in your thirties or forties . . . The same advice applies. Read some blogs hosted on different sites and pick one to join. There is no cost, and virtually no risk as you can always delete your blog if you later create a more sophisticated one. The only way to get better at blogging is to do it, so you might as well start today.

If you are in your fifties . . . Nothing is stopping you from setting up a blog right now; there are no age restrictions, except you may find the technology intimidating if you are not familiar with it. Again, just play around with the interface until you feel comfortable with it. There are various books, tutorials and help resources available to guide you through the set-up and posting process.

If you are over sixty . . . There are bloggers over sixty, but admittedly they are a small minority. Discomfort with using computers and sharing personal details online seems to rise with age. Readers of blogs also tend to be younger so your blog will have to have content that is intergenerationally appealing if you expect to attract a large following.

Further Resources

Blogger.com is the most popular free blog hosting service. http://www.blogger.com

Wordpress is a a provider of popular blogging software that you can download for free. You can also post a free blog at http://www.wordpress.com

Live Journal is a free blog hosting site that is popular with younger bloggers. It is used by bloggers of all ages, but its popularity has declined as other blog hosts have entered the market. http://www.livejournal.com

Become a Blogger.com provides video tutorials on WordPress as a blogging tool, as well as books and forums on becoming a blogger. http://becomeablogger.com

Day Trader

Career Compasses

Get your bearings on what it takes to be a successful day trader.

Relevant Knowledge of the stock market and online trading (40%)

Mathematical Skills are essential for any finance-related career (20%)

Organizational Skills are key to keeping track of your portfolio and investments (10%)

Ability to Manage Stress is absolutely crucial in this high-stress, high-pressure job (30%)

Destination: Day Trader

One obvious appeal of a career in day trading is that you can do it from anywhere in the world with Internet access. You need a computer, of course. A laptop is conveniently portable, but you will want as large a screen as possible. If you set up a fixed work station in your home or office, you will want multiple monitors so you do not have to waste valuable seconds switching between windows. You will need high-speed Internet access, as well as back-up access, such as a mobile phone with full Internet capabilities. A cable modem, DSL line, satellite, and a WiFi network are all appropriate options. (If you are considering day trading with a dial-up connection, close this book right now and smack yourself in the forehead with it.) You will also need to install some day trading software on your computer. There is software available for most operating systems, including Mac and Unix, but the largest variety of software is currently written for Windows XP; therefore, choosing Windows XP for your operating system will give you the widest choice of programs. Windows Vista would be a close second choice for compatibility, if necessary.

Since day traders handle all of their own trades, they have much less contact with their brokers than other types of investors, but they do need to have a relationship with a brokerage that they can contact if something goes wrong or their Internet connection goes down and they need to enter or exit a trade. Remember, this is a career in which seconds count and the disposition of large amounts of money depends upon speed and accuracy. So, make sure that you always have access to a telephone that is separate from your Internet connection when you are trading.

You will need to install some order entry software to place your trades. All trading software should give you the current and recent prices for each market, and should interface with some type of charting software so that you can see a graphical display of the market simultaneously. The software that you use will depend upon the day trading brokerage that you select. Each brokerage has its own software. In some cases, it comes free with your trading account, but some brokerages charge a monthly or yearly fee (anywhere from $50 to $1,000), which may be levied to everyone or only

Essential Gear

Do not be intimidated by terms. One would be hard-pressed to think of any other field that uses as many abbreviations and industry-specific terminology as the financial sector. The variety of financial instruments seems to increase so fast that not even the suppose experts who are working with them on a daily basis seem to understand them fully. If that seems implausible, consider the recent credit-default swaps scandal that brought down the banking industry worldwide in 2008. Before you start trading, be sure that you understand most of the terminology used to describe activity in financial markets. There are a lot of books available to help you get started, from *Day Trading for Dummies* (Ann C. Logue, For Dummies Press, 2007) to highly sophisticated market prognostications from self-proclaimed market gurus.

to those traders who do not make a minimum number of monthly trades and meet a commission threshold. Among the more popular day trading brokerages, Peregrine Financial Group uses Best Direct as their trading software; Transact Futures calls their package TransactAT; and, Interactive Brokers provides Trader Workstation (TWS) to its accountholders.

In addition to the trading software provided by your brokerage, you will probably want to install some additional front-end programs that can interface with your brokerage's software but that have some additional features and alternative displays. The ability to issue stop-loss and automatic target orders, for example, are features that you usually have to seek out additional software to get. Also, some trading software is easier to use than the brokerage-provided packages, so you may prefer to use it anyway. Popular third-party software includes Zero Line Trader, Auto Trader, Ninja Trader, and Bracket Trader. Some of these packages, such as Auto Trader, allow you to practice with simulated trades. As a neophyte trader, it is particularly important that you choose software with a demonstration mode that allows you to practice. Another reason that you may prefer to use third-party software is because you will spend much of your time watching the market via charts, and third-party charting software

Essential Gear

Get acquainted with market data. The continuous stream of real-time market data that will flow across your monitors is providing you with crucial information but it will not do you any good unless you can interpret it. Market data is divided into two levels. As a day trader, you will mostly be concerned about level 1 market data, which includes the bid price, the buy size, the ask price, the ask size, the last price, and the last size. Level 2 market data is sometimes called the order book as it includes all pending buy and sell orders for a given market, and it is also known as the market depth due to its listing of the number of contracts available at each buying and selling price. The information in level 2 market data includes the highest bid prices, the bid sizes, the lowest ask prices, and the ask sizes. Level 2 market data is generally more expensive because it provides additional information.

is generally superior to the charting software in brokerage-provided programs. The most widely used charting software packages are Quote Tracker, AmiBroker, Sierra Chart, Ensign Software, ESignal, and Trade-Maven. Charting software comes with a variety of display features and user interfaces, so play around with the demonstration version before you decide which one to purchase. There are three main types of charts: bar, candlestick, and line. You will need to be comfortable reading all of them. Each chart will also have parameters for the data it displays, either timeframe (a specific interval of time), ticks (number of trades), volume (number of contracts traded, which is more detailed than a tick chart because each trade can contain more than one contract), or price range. If you have programming skills, you can create your own trading software in your preferred programming language with exactly the features that you want it to possess.

Another major decision you will have to make before you begin your new career is which day trading brokerage to use. Day traders use direct access brokers rather than retail brokers because they need to be able to interface with their markets directly. The style, services, commission, reliability, provided software, and fees vary considerably between day trading brokerages, so do your research before you make a selection. Some of the more popular options include Interactive Brokers, TradeStation Securities, Transact Futures, NobleTrading, and Peregrine Financial Group. If you opt not to use a brokerage, you will need a direct trading account with each exchange, which is not very efficient or practical.

Finally, you will need a reliable source of real-time market data. As a day trader, delayed market data will do you no good; you need current pricing and volume information (that is, the number of contracts). This real-time data comes from the exchange that controls a given market and will be provided to you by your brokerage either gratis with an active trading account or for a fee. Recent historical market data should be included and archives of historical market data are available for purchase from each market's exchange. You should not need an additional source of market data other than that provided by your day trading brokerage; nonetheless, some traders like to have additional market data sources. Some popular alternative market data services include Track Data, OpenTick, ProRealTime, and DTN IQFeed. Monthly fees and user interfaces vary. Each one claims to be the fastest and most reliable so, you decide. Keep in mind that most brokerage provided software is only compatible with that particular brokerage's market data feed, so you will have to use third-party trading and charting software if you want to use a market data service other than the one provided by your brokerage. Most third party trading and charting software will be compatible with more than one market data feed.

You Are Here

You can begin your journey to day trading from many different locales.

Do you have financial sector experience? You do not need a degree in finance or a previous career on Wall Street to become a day trader, but it certainly helps. The more you know about the stock market, the better prepared you will be, and the more you will be able to decipher market data, understand what is happening in each market, and predict what is likely to happen in the near future. If you have experience in working in an investment firm, especially in fund management or equity investment, you are well-placed to start your own day trading business.

Do you have adequate risk capital? This is the key corollary to the previous question: Is it money that you can afford to lose? Like any skill with a steep learning curve, trading takes time to learn and you will make mistakes along the way. There are elements of skill, talent, and

Navigating the Terrain

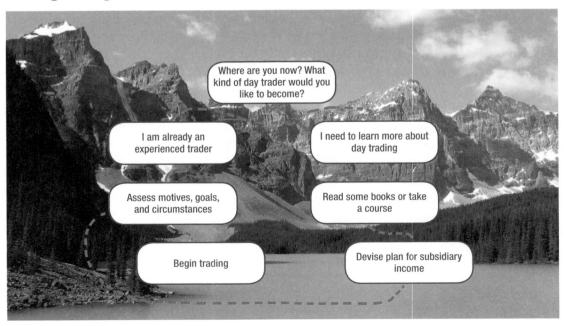

luck that together determine whether you will make or lose money and how much. You will not have the opportunity to learn from your (inevitable) mistakes if you lose all of the capital that you had to invest.

Do you have discipline? It takes a certain temperament to work as a day trader. You need to have a high tolerance for risk, but you also need to have the discipline to adhere to your strategy, tactics, and rules. If you buy on margin, you may have to force yourself to sell at a substantial loss to avoid an even more disastrous loss that could exceed your total assets. You need discipline not to overextend yourself and to resist the temptation to stay in to avoid losing part of your investment when all signs point to an even biggest loss if you wait.

Organizing Your Expedition

Before you set out, know where you are going.

Decide on a destination. Once you have gathered all of your brokerage tools, set up your workstation, and explored your software, you will need to make some major decisions about your day-trading business before you make your first trade. First and foremost, you need to decide which financial instruments you could like to trade. Stocks are the most common, but you could also trade stock options, currencies, or futures contracts, the most popular of which is commodity futures, although you can also trade equity index futures or interest rate futures.

Scout the terrain. Day traders employ many different strategies or trading methodologies to their work. Most day traders exit before the markets close each day to avoid overnight risks such as negative price gaps, hence the name. But a few traders will let the profits run. Others go to the opposite extreme and buy and sell every few minutes all day long. Brokerage firms like these traders because they get a commission on every trade, although most offer volume fee discounts to prolific traders. One particularly risky trading tactic is margin trading, in which the day trader borrows money to make trades. They avoid overnight interest charges on margin benefits by exiting before the closing bell, but they had better be right about the short-term direction of the price when they

Stories from the Field

Takashi Kotegawa
Day Trader
Tokyo, Japan

On December 8, 2005, a Japanese brokerage firm that meant to sell one share of the company J-Com Co for 610,000 yen made a slight typo and offered 610,000 shares at 1 yen apiece. The firm lost the equivalent of $347 million, but some individual day traders profited from the mistake, most notably Takashi Kotegawa. Under Japanese law, he and other individual day traders were not obligated to return their earnings. Many firms chose to do so anyway, but most individual traders refused, including Kotegawa, who had amassed the equivalent of $20 million in just ten minutes. This error was so serious and costly that the head of the Tokyo Stock Exchange was forced to resign. The Japanese media hounded Kotegawa for interviews after this incident, and he eventually agreed to appear on television. He is now somewhat of a celebrity in Japan. He started with about $13,600 and increased that to around $153 million over eight years. When the market crashed in 2008, he briefly adopted a cautious wait-and-see stance that he later regretted, but he came out all right in the end as he sold his holdings on the morning of an interest rate cut and made 400 million yen ($4.4 million) immediately.

are using borrowed money. You need to do a bit of research and devise your trading strategy before you dive into the markets. There are many books, courses and Web sites that are available to educate you on this subject.

Find the path that is right for you. It goes without saying that day trading is risky. Like any entrepreneurial venture, it may be awhile before you generate any income, you may want to plow that income right back into the business (i.e., reinvest it), or you may lose money. The most successful day traders earn millions of dollars per year, but the majority fail to even earn a living. You need to assess your personal financial situation and needs to be sure that you will be able to support yourself and your

Like many day traders, Kotegawa leads a spartan lifestyle that enables him to focus on the markets at all times. He says in all seriousness that, despite his wealth, he lives on ramen noodles so that he never has to be away from his computer and he is never so full that he is too sleepy to follow the markets diligently. He paid cash for a condominium that he uses as his trading headquarters. In Japan, Kotegawa is considered to be a hikikomori, that is, someone who has withdrawn socially and spends most of his time alone indoors. This is a similar phenomenon to agoraphobia and is sometimes linked with Asperger's syndrome. Although it is unfortunate to suffer from any social handicap, sometimes a handicap can be turned to an advantage. Videos on YouTube from a Japanese television interview with Kotegawa have been making the rounds of day trader message boards, and traders who have been studying his record strategy are quick to point out that he did not succeed based upon that one stoke of luck but, rather, because of his intense focus on the markets. He works at a small desk covered in computer monitors and strives not to be distracted from the numbers on the screens. Kotegawa admits the work is stressful but he has made enough money to get out of the business if he did not enjoy it enough to continue. Although he is in Japan, the global nature of modern financial markets makes his experience universally relevant to aspiring day traders. In the end, you make your own luck by never letting your attention waver.

family in a worst-case scenario of losing your money. The recent global market volatility should strike terror into every potential trader. This is not like starting an air conditioner repair business in Florida; making money is not assured even if you do everything right. You might want to start off as a casual trader and hold back on quitting your day job for awhile.

Go back to school. Since you are going into business for yourself, there are no credentials to submit to a potential employer. Day trading requires skills that are not taught in any degree program; however, there are plenty of courses and books, many available online, to help neophyte traders learn the business. The less you know about financial markets, the more you need to avail yourself of some of these resources. Just beware of scams. If someone is promising to teach you secrets that will enable you to get rich quick, it is likely to be the information age equivalent of a snake oil salesman. Legitimate educators will not make unrealistic promises. Generally, the larger the font and the more things blink, beep and pop up on the Web site, the less useful its information is likely to be.

Landmarks

If you are in your twenties . . . You can set yourself up as a day trader today if you want to, but you need to ensure that you have the time and interest to devote to this endeavor, and you need to maintain some perspective. You could fritter away your twenties in front of your computer without making a cent. Day trading can become an absorbing addiction, so be sure that you do not neglect other areas of your life at this crucial period in your social and intellectual development.

If you are in your thirties or forties . . . You may feel frustrated with the growth potential of other limitations of your current career and see day trading as your salvation. It is wise to do some research to ensure that your expectations for this career change are realistic and that you are able to meet your personal financial obligations and goals whilst you pursue it.

If you are in your fifties . . . Do not play around with your retirement savings. You may be concerned that you have not saved enough or that your investment portfolio is not performing as well as you would like, and you are growing concerned that you will not have enough money to retire when you want to (or at all). Thinking that you can secure your financial future through day trading is no different than thinking you can do it with a trip to Vegas or the purchase of a lottery ticket. Rein in your expectations. You may be able to make a career out of it, but start small and do not bet the farm.

If you are over sixty . . . You may be retired and looking for a second career or lucrative hobby. Day trading is a viable option as long as you have some money to burn. Do not be tempted to invest any of your retirement savings in the markets. Educate yourself, brush up your computer skills, and start slowly. You could make money but try to think of day trading as a hobby, at least at first.

Further Resources

Stockmaniacs is a day trader blog with a stock ticker and a live trading room. http://stockmaniacs.blogspot.com

Day Trading World is a general information Web site for neophyte day traders. http://www.daytradingworld.com

Securities and Exchange Commission Web page on day trading. http://www.sec.gov/answers/daytrading.htm

Financial Industry Regulatory Authority is the largest independent regulator of securities firms in the United States. Its role is to protect investors by ensuring market fairness. It was formed in 2007 as the result of a merger of two self-regulatory authorities: NYSE Regulation, Inc., and the National Association of Securities Dealers, Inc. (NASD). http://www.finra.org

Appendix A

Going Solo: Starting Your Own Business

Starting your own business can be very rewarding—not only in terms of potential financial success, but also in the pleasure derived from building something from the ground up, contributing to the community, being your own boss, and feeling reasonably in control of your fate. However, business ownership carries its own obligations—both in terms of long hours of hard work and new financial and legal responsibilities. If you succeed in growing your business, your responsibilities only increase. Many new business owners come in expecting freedom only to find themselves chained tighter to their desks than ever before. Still, many business owners find greater satisfaction in their career paths than do workers employed by others.

The Internet has also changed the playing field for small business owners, making it easier than ever before to strike out on your own. While small mom-and-pop businesses such as hairdressers and grocery stores have always been part of the economic landscape, the Internet has made reaching and marketing to a niche easier and more profitable. This has made possible a boom in *microbusinesses*. Generally, a microbusiness is considered to have under ten employees. A microbusiness is also sometimes called a *SoHo* for "small office/home office."

The following appendix is intended to explain, in general terms, the steps in launching a small business, no matter whether it is selling your Web-design services or opening a pizzeria with business partners. It will also point out some of the things you will need to bear in mind. Remember also that the particular obligations of your municipality, state, province, or country may vary, and that this is by no means a substitute for doing your own legwork. Further suggested reading is listed at the end.

Crafting a Business Plan

It has often been said that success is 1 percent inspiration and 99 percent perspiration. However, the interface between the two can often be hard to achieve. The first step to taking your idea and making it reality is constructing a viable *business plan*. The purpose of a business plan is to think things all the way through, to make sure your ideas really are

111

profitable, and to figure out the "who, what, when, where, why, and how" of your business. It fills in the details for three areas: your goals, why you think they are attainable, and how you plan to get to there. "You need to know where you're going before you take that first step," says Drew Curtis, successful Internet entrepreneur and founder of the popular newsfilter Fark.com.

Take care in writing your business plan. Generally, these documents contain several parts: An *executive summary* stating the essence of the plan; a *market summary* explaining how a need exists for the product and service you will supply and giving an idea of potential profitability by comparing your business to similar organizations; a *company description* which includes your products and services, why you think your organization will succeed, and any special advantages you have, as well as a description of *organization* and *management*; and your *marketing and sales strategy*. This last item should include market highlights and demographic information and trends that relate to your proposal. Also include a *funding request* for the amount of start-up capital you will need. This is supported by a section on *financials*, or the sort of cash flow you can expect, based on market analysis, projection, and comparison with existing companies. Other needed information, such as personal financial history, résumés, legal documents, or pictures of your product, can be placed in *appendices*.

Use your business plan to get an idea of how much startup money is necessary and to discipline your thinking and challenge your preconceived notions before you develop your cash flow. The business plan will tell you how long it will take before you turn a profit, which in turn is linked to how long it will before you will be able to pay back investors or a bank loan—which is something that anyone supplying you with money will want to know. Even if you are planning to subside on grants or you are not planning on investment or even starting a for-profit company, the discipline imposed by the business plan is still the first step to organizing your venture.

A business plan also gives you a realistic view of your personal financial obligations. How long can you afford to live without regular income? How are you going to afford medical insurance? When will your business begin turning a profit? How much of a profit? Will you need to reinvest your profits in the business, or can you begin living off of them? Proper planning is key to success in any venture.

A final note on business plans: Take into account realistic expected profit minus realistic costs. Many small business owners begin by underestimating start-ups and variable costs (such as electricity bills), and then underpricing their product. This effectively paints them into a corner from which it is hard to make a profit. Allow for realistic market conditions on both the supply and the demand side.

Partnering Up

You should think long and hard about the decision to go into business with a partner (or partners). Whereas other people can bring needed capital, expertise, and labor to a business, they can also be liabilities. The questions you need to ask yourself are:

☞ Will this person be a full and equal partner? In other words, are they able to carry their own weight? Make a full and fair assessment of your potential partner's personality. Going into business with someone who lacks a work ethic, or prefers giving directions to working in the trenches, can be a frustrating experience.

☞ What will they contribute to the business? For instance, a partner may bring in start-up money, facilities, or equipment. However, consider if this is enough of a reason to bring them on board. You may be able to get the same advantages in another way—for instance, renting a garage rather than working out of your partner's. Likewise, doubling skill sets does not always double productivity.

☞ Do they have any liabilities? For instance, if your prospective partner has declared bankruptcy in the past, this can hurt your collective venture's ability to get credit.

☞ Will the profits be able to sustain all the partners? Many start-up ventures do not turn profits immediately, and what little they do produce can be spread thin amongst many partners. Carefully work out the math.

Also bear in mind that going into business together can put a strain on even the best personal relationships. No matter whether it is family, friends, or strangers, keep everything very professional with written agreements regarding these investments. Get everything in writing, and be clear where obligations begin and end. "It's important to go into business with the right people," says Curtis. "If you don't—if it degrades into infighting and petty bickering—it can really go south quickly."

Incorporating. . . or Not

Think long and hard about incorporating. Starting a business often requires a fairly large—and risky—financial investment, which in turn exposes you to personal liability. Furthermore, as your business grows, so does your risk. Incorporating can help you shield yourself from this liability. However, it also has disadvantages.

To begin with, incorporating is not necessary for conducting professional transactions such as obtaining bank accounts and credit. You can do this as a sole proprietor, partnership, or simply by filing a DBA ("doing business as") statement with your local court (also known as "trading as" or an "assumed business name"). The DBA is an accounting entity that facilitates commerce and keeps your business' money separate from your own. However, the DBA does not shield you from responsibility if your business fails. It is entirely possible to ruin your credit, lose your house, and have your other assets seized in the unfortunate event of bankruptcy.

The purpose of incorporating is to shield yourself from personal financial liability. In case the worst happens, only the business' assets can be taken. However, this is not always the best solution. Check your local laws: Many states have laws that prevent a creditor from seizing a non-incorporated small business' assets in case of owner bankruptcy. If you are a corporation, however, the things you use to do business that are owned by the corporation—your office equipment, computers, restaurant refrigerators, and other essential equipment—may be seized by creditors, leaving you no way to work yourself out of debt. This is why it is imperative to consult with a lawyer.

There are other areas in which being a corporation can be an advantage, such as business insurance. Depending on your business needs, insurance can be for a variety of things: malpractice, against delivery failures or spoilage, or liability against defective products or accidents. Furthermore, it is easier to hire employees, obtain credit, and buy health insurance as an organization than as an individual. However, on the downside, corporations are subject to specific and strict laws concerning management and ownership. Again, you should consult with a knowledgeable legal expert.

Among the things you should discuss with your legal expert are the advantages and disadvantages of incorporating in your jurisdiction and which type of incorporation is best for you. The laws on liability and how much of your profit will be taken away in taxes vary widely by state and country. Generally, most small businesses owners opt for *limited liability companies* (LLCs), which gives them more control and a more flexible management structure. (Another possibility is a *limited liability partnership*, or *LLP*, which is especially useful for professionals such as doctors and lawyers.) Finally, there is the *corporation*, which is characterized by transferable ownerships shares, perpetual succession, and, of course, limited liability.

Most small businesses are sole proprietorships, partnerships, or privately-owned corporations. In the past, not many incorporated, since it was necessary to have multiple owners to start a corporation. However, this is changing, since it is now possible in many states for an individual to form a corporation. Note also that the form your business takes is usually not set in stone: A sole proprietorship or partnership can switch to become an LLC as it grows and the risks increase; furthermore, a successful LLC can raise capital by changing its structure to become a corporation and selling stock.

Legal Issues

Many other legal issues besides incorporating (or not) need to be addressed before you start your business. It is impossible to speak directly to every possible business need in this brief appendix, since regulations, licenses, and health and safety codes vary by industry and locality. A restaurant in Manhattan, for instance, has to deal not only with the usual issues such as health inspectors, the state liquor board, but obscure regulations such as New York City's cabaret laws, which prohibit dancing without a license in a place where alcohol is sold. An asbestos-abatement company, on the other hand, has a very different set of standards it has to abide by, including federal regulations. Researching applicable laws is part of starting up any business.

Part of being a wise business owner is knowing when you need help. There is software available for things like bookkeeping, business plans, and Web site creation, but generally, consulting with a knowledgeable professional—an accountant or a lawyer (or both)—is the smartest move. One of the most common mistakes is believing that just because you have expertise in the technical aspects of a certain field, you know all about running a business in that field. Whereas some people may balk at the expense, by suggesting the best way to deal with possible problems, as well as cutting through red tape and seeing possible pitfalls that you may not even have been aware of, such professionals usually more than make up for their cost. After all, they have far more experience at this than does a first-time business owner!

Financial

Another necessary first step in starting a business is obtaining a bank account. However, having the account is not as important as what you do with it. One of the most common problems with small businesses is undercapitalization—especially in brick-and-mortar businesses that sell or make something, rather than service-based businesses. The rule of thumb is that you should have access to money equal to your first year's anticipated profits, plus start-up expenses. (Note that this is not the same as having the money on hand—see the discussion on lines of credit, below.) For instance, if your annual rent, salaries, and equipment will cost $50,000 and you expect $25,000 worth of profit in your first year, you should have access to $75,000 worth of financing.

You need to decide what sort of financing you will need. Small business loans have both advantages and disadvantages. They can provide critical start-up credit, but in order to obtain one, your personal credit will need to be good, and you will, of course, have to pay them off with interest. In general, the more you and your partners put into the business yourselves, the more credit lenders will be willing to extend to you.

Equity can come from your own personal investment, either in cash or an equity loan on your home. You may also want to consider bringing on partners—at least limited financial partners—as a way to cover start-up costs.

It is also worth considering obtaining a line of credit instead of a loan. A loan is taken out all at once, but with a line of credit, you draw on the money as you need it. This both saves you interest payments and means that you have the money you need when you need it. Taking out too large of a loan can be worse than having no money at all! It just sits there collecting interest—or, worse, is spent on something utterly unnecessary—and then is not around when you need it most.

The first five years are the hardest for any business venture; your venture has about double the usual chance of closing in this time (1 out of 6, rather than 1 out of 12). You will probably have to tighten your belt at home, as well as work long hours and keep careful track of your business expenses. Be careful with your money. Do not take unnecessary risks, play it conservatively, and always keep some capital in reserve for emergencies. The hardest part of a new business, of course, is the learning curve of figuring out what, exactly, you need to do to make a profit, and so the best advice is to have plenty of savings—or a job to provide income—while you learn the ropes.

One thing you should not do is count on venture capitalists or "angel investors," that is, businesspeople who make a living investing on other businesses in the hopes that their equity in the company will increase in value. Venture capitalists have gotten something of a reputation as indiscriminate spendthrifts due to some poor choices made during the dot-com boom of the late 1990s, but the fact is that most do not take risks on unproven products. Rather, they are attracted to young companies that have the potential to become regional or national powerhouses and give better-than-average returns. Nor are venture capitalists are endless sources of money; rather, they are savvy businesspeople who are usually attracted to companies that have already experienced a measure of success. Therefore, it is better to rely on your own resources until you have proven your business will work.

Bookkeeping 101

The principles of double-entry bookkeeping have not changed much since its invention in the fifteenth century: one column records debits, and one records credits. The trick is *doing* it. As a small business owner, you need to be disciplined and meticulous at recording your finances. Thankfully, today there is software available that can do everything from tracking payables and receivables to running checks and generating reports.

Honestly ask yourself if you are the sort of person who does a good job keeping track of finances. If you are not, outsource to a bookkeeping company or hire someone to come in once or twice a week to enter invoices and generate checks for you. Also remember that if you have employees or even freelancers, you will have to file tax forms for them at the end of the year.

Another good idea is to have an accountant for your business to handle advice and taxes (federal, state, local, sales tax, etc.). In fact, consulting with an a certified public accountant is a good idea in general, since they are usually aware of laws and rules that you have never even heard of.

Finally, keep your personal and business accounting separate. If your business ever gets audited, the first thing the IRS looks for is personal expenses disguised as business expenses. A good accountant can help you to know what are legitimate business expenses. Everything you take from the business account, such as payroll and reimbursement, must be recorded and classified.

Being an Employer

Know your situation regarding employees. To begin with, if you have any employees, you will need an Employer Identification Number (EIN), also sometimes called a Federal Tax Identification Number. Getting an EIN is simple: You can fill out IRS form SS-4, or complete the process online at http://www.irs.gov.

Having employees carries other responsibilities and legalities with it. To begin with, you will need to pay payroll taxes (otherwise known as "withholding") to cover income tax, unemployment insurance, Social Security, and Medicare, as well as file W-2 and W-4 forms with the government. You will also be required to pay workman's compensation insurance, and will probably also want to find medical insurance. You are also required to abide by your state's nondiscrimination laws. Most states require you to post nondiscrimination and compensation notices in a public area.

Many employers are tempted to unofficially hire workers "off the books." This can have advantages, but can also mean entering a legal gray area. (Note, however, this is different from hiring freelancers, a temp employed by another company, or having a self-employed professional such as an accountant or bookkeeper come in occasionally to provide a service.) It is one thing to hire the neighbor's teenage son on a one-time basis to help you move some boxes, but quite another to have full-time workers working on a cash-and-carry basis. Regular wages must be noted in the accounts, and gaps may be questioned in the event of an audit. If the workers are injured on the job, you are not covered by workman's comp, and are thus vulnerable to lawsuits. If the workers you hired are not legal residents, you can also be liable for civil and criminal penalties. In general, it is best to keep your employees as above-board as possible.

Building a Business

Good business practices are essential to success. First off, do not overextend yourself. Be honest about what you can do and in what time frame. Secondly, be a responsible business owner. In general, if there is a problem, it is best to explain matters honestly to your clients than to leave them without word and wondering. In the former case, there is at least the possibility of salvaging your reputation and credibility.

Most business is still built by personal contacts and word of mouth. It is for this reason that maintaining your list of contacts is an essential practice. Even if a particular contact may not be useful at a particular moment, a future opportunity may present itself—or you may be able to send someone else to them. Networking, in other words, is as important when you are the boss as when you are looking for a job yourself. As the owner of a company, having a network means getting services on better terms, knowing where to go if you need help with a particular problem, or simply being in the right place at the right time to exploit an opportunity. Join professional organizations, the local Chamber of Commerce, clubs and community organizations, and learn to play golf. And remember—never burn a bridge.

Advertising is another way to build a business. Planning an ad campaign is not as difficult as you might think: You probably already know your media market and business community. The trick is applying it. Again, go with your instincts. If you never look twice at your local weekly, other people probably do not, either. If you are in a high-tourist area, though, local tourists maps might be a good way to leverage your marketing dollar. Ask other people in your area or market who have business similar to your own. Depending on your focus, you might want to consider everything from AM radio or local TV networks, to national trade publications, to hiring a PR firm for an all-out blitz. By thinking about these questions, you can spend your advertising dollars most effectively.

Nor should you underestimate the power of using the Internet to build your business. It is a very powerful tool for small businesses, potentially reaching vast numbers of people for relatively little outlay of money. Launching a Web site has become the modern equivalent of hanging out your shingle. Even if you are primarily a brick-and-mortar business, a Web presence can still be an invaluable tool—your store or offices will show up on Google searches, plus customers can find directions to visit you in person. Furthermore, the Internet offers the small-business owner many useful tools. Print and design services, order fulfillment, credit card processing, and networking—both personal and in terms of linking to other sites—are all available online. Web advertising can be useful, too, either by advertising on specialty sites that appeal to your audience, or by using services such as Google AdWords.

Amateurish print ads, TV commercials, and Web sites do not speak well of your business. Good media should be well-designed, well-edited, and well-put together. It need not, however, be expensive. Shop around and, again, use your network.

Flexibility is also important. "In general, a business must adapt to changing conditions, find new customers and find new products or services that customers need when the demand for their older products or services diminishes," says James Peck, a Long Island, New York, entrepreneur. In other words, if your original plan is not working out, or if demand falls, see if you can parlay your experience, skills, and physical plant into meeting other needs. People are not the only ones who can change their path in life; organizations can, too.

A Final Word

In business, as in other areas of life, the advice of more experienced people is essential. "I think it really takes three businesses until you know what you're doing," Drew Curtis confides. "I sure didn't know what I was doing the first time." Listen to what others have to say, no matter whether it is about your Web site or your business plan. One possible solution is seeking out a mentor, someone who has previously launched a successful venture in this field. In any case, before taking any step, ask as many people as many questions as you can. Good advice is invaluable.

Further Resources

American Independent Business Alliance
http://www.amiba.net

American Small Business League
http://www.asbl.com

IRS Small Business and Self-Employed One-Stop Resource
http://www.irs.gov/businesses/small/index.html

The Riley Guide: Steps in Starting Your Own Business
http://www.rileyguide.com/steps.html

Small Business Administration
http://www.sba.gov

Appendix B

Outfitting Yourself for Career Success

As you contemplate a career shift, the first component is to assess your interests. You need to figure out what makes you tick, since there is a far greater chance that you will enjoy and succeed in a career that taps into your passions, inclinations, natural abilities, and training. If you have a general idea of what your interests are, you at least know in which direction you want to travel. You may know you want to simply switch from one sort of nursing to another, or change your life entirely and pursue a dream you have always held. In this case, you can use a specific volume of The Field Guides to Finding a New Career to discover which position to target. If you are unsure of your direction you want to take, well, then the entire scope of the series is open to you! Browse through to see what appeals to you, and see if it matches with your experience and abilities.

The next step you should take is to make a list—do it once in writing—of the skills you have used in a position of responsibility that transfer to the field you are entering. People in charge of interviewing and hiring may well understand that the skills they are looking for in a new hire are used in other fields, but you must spell it out. Most job descriptions are partly a list of skills. Map your experience into that, and very early in your contacts with a prospective employer explicitly address how you acquired your relevant skills. Pick a relatively unimportant aspect of the job to be your ready answer for where you would look forward to learning within the organization, if this seems essentially correct. When you transfer into a field, softly acknowledge a weakness while relating your readiness to learn, but never lose sight of the value you offer both in your abilities and in the freshness of your perspective.

Energy and Experience

The second component in career-switching success is energy. When Jim Fulmer was 61, he found himself forced to close his piano-repair business. However, he was able to parlay his knowledge of music, pianos, and the musical instruments industry into another job as a sales representative for a large piano manufacturer, and quickly built up a clientele of

125

musical-instrument retailers throughout the East Coast. Fulmer's experience highlights another essential lesson for career-changers: There are plenty of opportunities out there, but jobs will not come to you—especially the career-oriented, well-paying ones. You have to seek them out.

Jim Fulmer's case also illustrates another important point: Former training and experience can be a key to success. "Anyone who has to make a career change in any stage of life has to look at what skills they have acquired but may not be aware of," he says. After all, people can more easily change into careers similar to the ones they are leaving. Training and experience also let you enter with a greater level of seniority, provided you have the other necessary qualifications. For instance, a nurse who is already experienced with administering drugs and their benefits and drawbacks, and who is also graced with the personality and charisma to work with the public, can become a pharmaceutical company sales representative.

Unlock Your Network

The next step toward unlocking the perfect job is networking. The term may be overused, but the idea is as old as civilization. More than other animals, humans need one another. With the Internet and telephone, never in history has it been easier to form (or revive) these essential links. One does not have to gird oneself and attend reunion-type events (though for many this is a fine tactic)—but keep open to opportunities to meet people who may be friendly to you in your field. Ben Franklin understood the principal well—*Poor Richard's Almanac* is something of a treatise on the importance or cultivating what Franklin called "friendships" with benefactors. So follow in the steps of the founding fathers and make friends to get ahead. Remember: helping others feels good; it's often the receiving that gets a little tricky. If you know someone particularly well-connected in your field, consider tapping one or two less important connections first so that you make the most of the important one. As you proceed, keep your strengths foremost in your mind because the glue of commerce is mutual interest.

Eighty percent of job openings are *never advertised*, and, according to the U.S. Bureau of Labor statistics, more than half all employees landed their jobs through networking. Using your personal contacts is far more efficient and effective than trusting your résumé to the Web. On the Web, an employer needs to sort through tens of thousands—or millions—of résumés. When you direct your application to one potential employer, you are directing your inquiry to one person who already knows you. The personal touch is everything: Human beings are social animals, programmed to "read" body language; we are naturally inclined to trust those we meet in person, or who our friends and coworkers have recommended. While Web sites can be useful (for looking through help-wanted ads, for instance), expecting employers to pick you out of the slush pile is as effective as throwing your résumé into a black hole.

Do not send your résumé out just to make yourself feel like you're doing something. The proper way to go about things is to employ discipline and order, and then to apply your charm. Begin your networking efforts by making a list of people you can talk to: colleagues, coworkers, and supervisors, people you have had working relationship with, people from church, athletic teams, political organizations, or other community groups, friends, and relatives. You can expand your networking opportunities by following the suggestions in each chapter of the volumes. Your goal here is not so much to land a job as to expand your possibilities and knowledge: Though the people on your list may not be in the position to help you themselves, they might know someone who is. Meeting with them might also help you understand traits that matter and skills that are valued in the field in which you are interested. Even if the person is a potential employer, it is best to phrase your request as if you were seeking information: "You might not be able to help me, but do you know someone I could talk to who could tell me more about what it is like to work in this field?" Being hungry gives one impression, being desperate quite another.

Keep in mind that networking is a two-way street. If you meet someone who had an opening that is not right for you, but if you could recommend someone else, you have just added to your list two people who will be favorably disposed toward you in the future. Also, bear in mind that *you* can help people in *your* old field, thus adding to your own contacts list.

Networking is especially important to the self-employed or those who start their own businesses. Many people in this situation begin because they either recognize a potential market in a field that they are familiar with, or because full-time employment in this industry is no longer a possibility. Already being well-established in a field can help, but so can asking connections for potential work and generally making it known that you are ready, willing, and able to work. Working your professional connections, in many cases, is the *only* way to establish yourself. A free-lancer's network, in many cases, is like a spider's web. The spider casts out many strands, since he or she never knows which one might land the next meal.

Dial-Up Help

In general, it is better to call contacts directly than to e-mail them. E-mails are easy for busy people to ignore or overlook, even if they do not mean to. Explain your situation as briefly as possible (see the discussion of the "elevator speech"), and ask if you could meet briefly, either at their office or at a neutral place such as a café. (Be sure that you pay the bill in such a situation—it is a way of showing you appreciate their time and effort.) If you get someone's voicemail, give your "elevator speech" and then say you will call back in a few days to follow up—and then do so. If you reach your contact directly and they are too busy to speak or meet with you, make a definite appointment to call back at a later date. Be persistent, but not annoying.

Once you have arranged a meeting, prep yourself. Look at industry publications both in print and online, as well as news reports (here, GoogleNews, which lets you search through online news reports, can be very handy). Having up-to-date information on industry trends shows that you are dedicated, knowledgeable, and focused. Having specific questions on employers and requests for suggestions will set you apart from the rest of the job-hunting pack. Knowing the score—for instance, asking about the value of one sort of certification instead of another—pegs you as an "insider," rather than a dilettante, someone whose name is worth remembering and passing along to a potential employer.

Finally, set the right mood. Here, a little self-hypnosis goes a long way: Look at yourself in the mirror, and tell yourself that you are an enthusiastic, committed professional. Mood affects confidence and performance. Discipline your mind so you keep your perspective and self-respect. Nobody wants to hire someone who comes across as insincere, tells a sob story, or is still in the doldrums of having lost their previous job. At the end of any networking meeting, ask for someone else who might be able to help you in your journey to finding a position in this field, either with information or a potential job opening.

Get a Lift

When you meet with a contact in person (as well as when you run into anyone by chance who may be able to help you), you need an "elevator speech" (so-named because it should be short enough to be delivered during an elevator ride from a ground level to a high floor). This is a summary in which, in less than two minutes, you give them a clear impression of who you are, where you come from, your experience and goals, and why you are on the path you are on. The motto above Plato's Academy holds true: Know Thyself (this is where our Career Compasses and guides will help you). A long and rambling "elevator story" will get you nowhere. Furthermore, be positive: Neither a sad-sack story nor a tirade explaining how everything that went wrong in your old job is someone else's fault will get you anywhere. However, an honest explanation of a less-than-fortunate circumstance, such as a decline in business forcing an office closing, needing to change residence to a place where you are not qualified to work in order to further your spouse's career, or needing to work fewer hours in order to care for an ailing family member, is only honest.

An elevator speech should show 1) you know the business involved; 2) you know the company; 3) you are qualified (here, try to relate your education and work experience to the new situation); and 4) you are goal-oriented, dependable, and hardworking. Striking a balance is important; you want to sound eager, but not overeager. You also want to show a steady work experience, but not that you have been so narrowly focused that you cannot adjust. Most important is emphasizing what you can do for the company. You will be surprised how much information you can include in two minutes. Practice this speech in front of a mirror until you have the key points down perfectly. It should sound natural, and you should come across as friendly, confident, and assertive. Finally, remember eye contact! Good eye contact needs to be part of your presentation, as well as your everyday approach when meeting potential employers and leads.

Get Your Résumé Ready

Everyone knows what a résumé is, but how many of us have really thought about how to put one together? Perhaps no single part of the job search is subject to more anxiety—or myths and misunderstandings—than this 8 ½-by-11-inch sheet of paper.

On the one hand, it is perfectly all right for someone—especially in certain careers, such as academia—to have a résumé that is more than one page. On the other hand, you do not need to tell a future employer *everything*. Trim things down to the most relevant; for a 40-year-old to mention an internship from two decades ago is superfluous. Likewise, do not include irrelevant jobs, lest you seem like a professional career-changer.

Tailor your descriptions of your former employment to the particular position you are seeking. This is not to say you should lie, but do make your experience more appealing. If the job you're looking for involves supervising other people, say if you have done this in the past; if it involves specific knowledge or capabilities, mention that you possess these qualities. In general, try to make your past experience seem as similar to what you are seeking.

The standard advice is to put your Job Objective at the heading of the résumé. An alternative to this is a Professional Summary, which some recruiters and employers prefer. The difference is that a Job Objective mentions the position you are seeking, whereas a Professional Summary mentions your background (e.g. "Objective: To find a position as a sales representative in agribusiness machinery" versus "Experienced sales representative; strengths include background in agribusiness, as well as building team dynamics and market expansion"). Of course, it is easy to come up with two or three versions of the same document for different audiences.

The body of the résumé of an experienced worker varies a lot more than it does at the beginning of your career. You need not put your education or your job experience first; rather, your résumé should emphasize your strengths. If you have a master's degree in a related field, that might want to go before your unrelated job experience. Conversely, if too much education will harm you, you might want to bury that under the section on professional presentations you have given that show how good you are at communicating. If you are currently enrolled in a course or other professional development, be sure to note this (as well as your date of expected graduation). A résumé is a study of blurs, highlights, and jewels. You blur everything you must in order to fit the description of your experience to the job posting. You highlight what is relevant from each and any of your positions worth mentioning. The jewels are the little headers and such—craft them, since they are what is seen first.

You may also want to include professional organizations, work-related achievements, and special abilities, such as your fluency in a foreign language. Also mention your computer software qualifications and capabilities, especially if you are looking for work in a technological field or if you are an older job-seeker who might be perceived as behind the technology curve. Including your interests or family information might or might not be a good idea—no one really cares about your bridge club, and in fact they might worry that your marathon training might take away from your work commitments, but, on the other hand, mentioning your golf handicap or three children might be a good idea if your potential employer is an avid golfer or is a family woman herself.

You can either include your references or simply note, "References available upon request." However, be sure to ask your references' permission to use their names and alert them to the fact that they may be contacted before you include them on your résumé! Be sure to include name, organization, phone number, and e-mail address for each contact.

Today, word processors make it easy to format your résumé. However, beware of prepackaged résumé "wizards"—they do not make you stand out in the crowd. Feel free to strike out on your own, but remember the most important thing in formatting a résumé is consistency. Unless you have a background in typography, do not get too fancy. Finally, be sure to have someone (or several people!) read your résumé over for you.

For more information on résumé writing, check out Web sites such as http://www.résumé.monster.com.

Craft Your Cover Letter

It is appropriate to include a cover letter with your résumé. A cover letter lets you convey extra information about yourself that does not fit or is not always appropriate in your résumé, such as why you are no longer working in your original field of employment. You can and should also mention the name of anyone who referred you to the job. You can go into some detail about the reason you are a great match, given the job description. Also address any questions that might be raised in the potential employer's mind (for instance, a gap in employment). Do not, however, ramble on. Your cover letter should stay focused on your goal: To offer a strong, positive impression of yourself and persuade the hiring manager that you are worth an interview. Your cover letter gives you a chance to stand out from the other applicants and sell yourself. In fact, according to a CareerBuilder.com survey, 23 percent of hiring managers say a candidate's ability to relate his or her experience to the job at hand is a top hiring consideration.

Even if you are not a great writer, you can still craft a positive yet concise cover letter in three paragraphs: An introduction containing the specifics of the job you are applying for; a summary of why you are a good fit for the position and what you can do for the company; and a closing with a request for an interview, contact information, and thanks. Remember to vary the structure and tone of your cover letter—do not begin every sentence with "I."

Ace Your Interview

In truth, your interview begins well before you arrive. Be sure to have read up well on the company and its industry. Use Web sites and magazines—http://www.hoovers.com offers free basic business information, and trade magazines deliver both information and a feel for the industries they cover. Also, do not neglect talking to people in your circle who might know about trends in the field. Leave enough time to digest the information so that you can give some independent thought to the company's history and prospects. You don't need to expert when you arrive to be interviewed; but you should be comfortable. The most important element of all is to be poised and relaxed during the interview itself. Preparation and practice can help a lot.

Be sure to develop well-thought-through answers to the following, typical interview openers and standard questsions.

☞ Tell me about yourself. (Do not complain about how unsatisfied you were in your former career, but give a brief summary of your applicable background and interest in the particular job area.) If there is a basis to it, emphasize how much you love to work and how you are a team player.

☞ Why do you want this job? (Speak from the brain, and the heart—of course you want the money, but say a little here about what you find interesting about the field and the company's role in it.)

☞ What makes you a good hire? (Remember here to connect the company's needs and your skill set. Ultimately, your selling points probably come down to one thing: you will make your employer money. You want the prospective hirer to see that your skills are valuable not to the world in general but to this specific company's bottom line. What can you do for them?)

☞ What led you to leave your last job? (If you were fired, still try say something positive, such as, "The business went through a challenging time, and some of the junior marketing people were let go.")

Practice answering these and other questions, and try to be genuinely positive about yourself, and patient with the process. Be secure but not cocky; don't be shy about forcing the focus now and then on positive contributions you have made in your working life—just be specific. As with the elevator speech, practice in front of the mirror.

A couple pleasantries are as natural a way as any to start the actual interview, but observe the interviewer closely for any cues to fall silent and formally begin. Answer directly; when in doubt, finish your phrase and look to the interviewer. Without taking command, you can always ask, "Is there more you would like to know?" Your attentiveness will convey respect. Let your personality show too—a positive attitude and a grounded sense of your abilities will go a long way to getting you considered. During the interview, keep your cell phone off and do not look at your watch. Toward the end of your meeting, you may be asked whether you have any questions. It is a good idea to have one or two in mind. A few examples follow:

☞ "What makes your company special in the field?"
☞ "What do you consider the hardest part of this position?"
☞ "Where are your greatest opportunities for growth?"
☞ "Do you know when you might need anything further from me?"

Leave discussion of terms for future conversations. Make a cordial, smooth exit.

Remember to Follow Up

Send a thank-you note. Employers surveyed by CareerBuilder.com in 2005 said it matters. About 15 percent said they would not hire someone who did not follow up with a thanks. And almost 33 percent would think less of a candidate. The form of the note does not much matter—if you know a manager's preference, use it. Otherwise, just be sure to follow up.

Winning an Offer

A job offer can feel like the culmination of a long and difficult struggle. So naturally, when you hear them, you may be tempted to jump at the offer. Don't. Once an employer wants you, he or she will usually give you a chance to consider the offer. This is the time to discuss terms of employment, such as vacation, overtime, and benefits. A little effort now can be well worth it in the future. Be sure to do a check of prevailing salaries for your field and area before signing on. Web sites for this include Payscale.com, Salary.com, and Salaryexpert.com. If you are thinking about asking for better or different terms from what the prospective employer offered, rest assured—that's how business gets done; and it may just burnish the positive impression you have already made.

Index